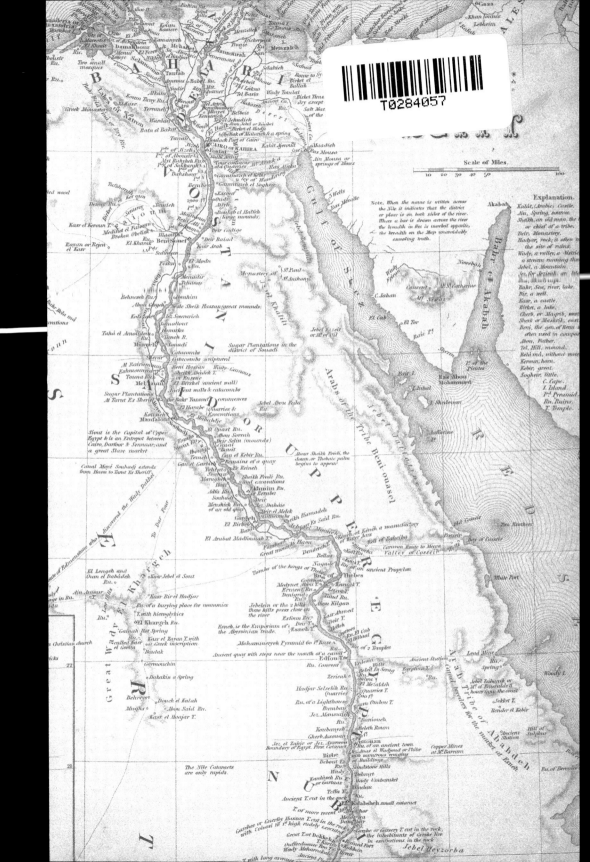

CAMELS, TOMBS AND PAINTED ROOMS

Adventures in Egypt with Flashlights and TP

MARY W. SCHALLER

ISBN 979-8-35096-552-0

"As for him who knows this book, nothing evil shall have power over him;

He shall not be turned away from the gates of the West;

He shall go in and out;

And bread and beer and all good things shall be given to him in the presence

Of those who are in the Netherworld.

— Spell 181

Egyptian Book of the Dead

Mary & Marty Schaller in the Kitchener Gardens, Aswan

Dedication

To our Merry Band of Fellow Travelers

February 21 – March 2, 1992

The Temple of Horus the Falcon God at Edfu.

L to R, Back Row: Mohammed, Betty, Mary, Fred, Craig, Griff, George, Harriet, Vic, Joyce, Av, Carol, Norm, Helen, Bill, Joy & Rick.

L to R, Seated: Polly, Ginger, Marty, Mary S., Gladys, Sandi, Vin & Dale

CONTENTS

CHAPTER ONE

"NOT THAT HAT!"

In the Autumn of 1991, two incredible things happened to the Schaller family. Our daughter, Tori, announced her engagement to marry her boyfriend, Rick, and I inherited a windfall legacy from an elderly second cousin in Kentucky. Both events were entirely unexpected.

"Good grief, Schaller!" gasped my husband, Marty, who tended to use our last name in moments of extreme emotion. He held up the check from my cousin's lawyer which had just arrived in the mail. "Do you realize that we could completely re-do the kitchen, and carpet the entire house with this? Or —"

He paused and looked at me. Then he smiled. "Or we could give Tori the Wedding of the Century, and then you and I could go on a trip – down the Nile in Egypt!"

I didn't need a minute to consider the choices. Both of us, being romantic, young at heart and only slightly crazy, agreed on the latter course of action.

The following day, Marty made a long visit with a travel agent. He came home with dozens of glossy brochures filled with color photos of pyramids, camels, pharaohs, and lots of exotic-looking palm trees. Meanwhile, our daughter bought at least seven different bridal magazines. Our son, Phil, who is a professional chef, retreated to his kitchen in self – preservation.

I dashed off to the local library and checked out Egypt – all of it. Marty made up graphs and charts, highlighting each travel company's packaged tour to the Land of Pyramids: ten glorious days, fifteen glorious days, twenty glorious days aboard Nile cruisers. There were backpack and felucca boat tours; tours by camel; tours with an optional safari in Kenya; tours that included a visit to Israel; tours by hot air balloons; scuba-diving tours in the Red Sea and archeological digging tours, et al. The choices were mind-boggling.

Tori made up wedding invitation lists, Bridal Registry lists, monthly check-off lists, and shopping lists.

Phil researched wedding cake recipes.

Meanwhile, I read through Discovery guides, Berlitz guides, Forder guides, Mark Twain's Innocents Abroad; Flaubert in Egypt; books by mystery writers Agatha Christie and Elizabeth Peters; The Mummy by Anne Rice; two separate translations of The Egyptian Book of The Dead; The Rubaiyat of Omar Khayyam; The 1001 Arabian Nights; a medium-sized book about What The Mother-of-the-Bride Should Know, [Basically, it was 205 pages that said "Stay Calm".] and last, but never least, the Bible.

Considering all our upcoming expenses, we chose the Ten Glorious Days in Egypt Tour with five of those days aboard a Nile River Cruise boat. Sphinx, Pyramids, King Tut's tomb, Abu Simbel, camels — it was all ours for an immediate twenty percent deposit. Marty signed on the dotted line, then sent off our applications for visas. Tori narrowed her wedding guest list to one-hundred-and-fifty nearest and dearest. I ordered wedding invitations and borrowed training films from the local video store: *Father of the Bride, Death on the Nile, Lawrence of Arabia, Betsey's Wedding,* and *Raiders of the Lost Ark.* Phil experimented with various wedding cake recipes, searched for Mexican Day of the Dead bride and groom figures for the cake topper [please don't ask!], selected the reception menu and managed to keep a very, very low profile.

In early December 1991, Tori and Rick had their wedding with all the trimmings, and they departed on their honeymoon cruise to the Caribbean. Phil breathed a sigh of relief, gave us his Egyptian wish list, and returned to his restaurant. Meanwhile, Marty made several doctor's appointments for — inoculations.

I have nothing against our doctor. He is a kind, gentle man. I just hate seeing him professionally when he's holding a needle in his hand — in this case, several needles. To start, he lectured us on the perils of touching, much less drinking the water from the Nile. Also, he warned us not to pet anything cute, furry or that has scales. He loaded us up with pills for malaria and traveler's tummy, then he shot us up with vaccines for hepatitis A, hepatitis B, typhoid, yellow fever, polio, rabies, tetanus, and wicked-looking vials of something yellowish called gamma globulin.

"Now, don't you feel like you are really going on an adventure?" asked my sadistic husband with a little smile. He knew how much I hated shots. Meanwhile the nurse prepared a huge needle that looked like it could be used to calm large, obnoxious horses.

"No!" I snarled through gritted teeth as the globs of gamma oozed through the hole in my hip. "I feel like I'm going to faint."

Which I did.

In retaliation for the visit to the doctor's office, I did the only thing any rational woman with a sudden, large expense account would do. I went shopping, spreading joy and VISA plastic among the collected merchants of our local shopping mall. After all, we were going to Egypt, and I needed to be properly outfitted: khaki pants, cotton shirts, desert boots, suntan lotion, pocket flashlights, camper's TP, and the one article that every self-respecting explorer should have.

"Don't tell me that you are planning to wear that . . . that . . . that hat in Egypt, are you?" Marty's face turned a shade red at the sight of it.

I clutched the article in question to my bosom. "Of course, I am! It's perfect!"

Marty curled his lip in disgust. "You'll never be able to pack that thing. It'll get crushed" He sounded hopeful.

"Oh, I don't intend to pack it." I smiled sweetly at him. "I intend to wear it."

"On the plane?" Marty gasped, then turned a little pale.

"Of course!"

My white straw pith helmet with adjustable terry cloth sweat band did indeed survive the twenty-seven-hour trip to Glorious Egypt. In fact, that hat and the camper's TP were the two smartest purchases I had made for our upcoming adventure

CHAPTER TWO

FIRST IMPRESSIONS

We came to Egypt to see the Old – and we found ourselves surrounded by the Modern: the traffic, the noise, and the hustle and
bustle of Cairo, a capital city of nine and a half million people,
who carried on with the business of daily living.

And yet, the Old prevailed all around us. In a corner vegetable market
that was the size of an American guest room closet, enormous, bright orange
carrots, the type found only in Rabbit Heaven, were stacked shoulder high.
Amid the swirling, unceasing street traffic, tired, under-appreciated little
donkeys pulled huge loads without a flick of their ears at the cars honking
behind them. A wedding procession burst through an intersection – stopping traffic in all directions. Almost every day, someone gets married in
Cairo. This day's joyful, colorful parade was the bride's new furniture which
the groom's friends had stacked on pickup trucks enroute to the couple's new
home. The groom, in the lead vehicle, was anxious to show the whole world
the beautiful things he had chosen for his new bride. A lot of handclapping,
music and puffed-up strutting accompanied the tables, chairs and rolled up
rugs that inched their way through the crowded streets. Cars honked, people
on the sidewalks waved, and everyone laughed or shrugged at the sight.

In a clean-swept Cairo carpet factory, beautiful young children, their large eyes looking like melting chocolate, bent over the bright-colored looms. Their tiny fingers flew so fast over the threads that they become a blur. It hurt my heart to realize that these talented young weavers, who should have been in elementary school, were the real breadwinners for their families.

A bored-looking soldier, astride a patient camel, was armed with a wicked-looking bullwhip and a submachine gun. He was the traffic cop, and he did not look like the type of guy you could talk out of a parking ticket. In the fields that bordered the city, long-horned bullocks plowed the damp, black earth exactly as their ancestors have done for the past five millennium.

Religion is the cornerstone in Egypt. It was six o'clock in the evening, when Marty and I arrived inside the Cairo International Airport, after a day and a half of air travel. While waiting for our hotel's van driver to come claim us, I decided to buy some Egyptian postcards to send home to our kids to let them know that we had arrived safely. However, the brightly lit postcard stall in the center of the airport's concourse looked empty. In this country of the twenty-four-hour sales pitch, there was no salesman behind the counter, waiting to overcharge me for several dusty postcards. Instead, he was kneeling devoutly, head down, on a piece of tattered cardboard behind the counter. While facing the sacred city of Mecca, he prayed to Allah. We, his potential customers from several different countries, waited in respectful silence for him to finish. I tried to imagine a shop keeper praying to Mecca in the middle of Chicago's O'Hare terminal. Impossible!

On the way to our hotel in the early darkness of a February evening, our van driver demonstrated a few hair-raising Egyptian driving techniques as he navigated through the infamous Cairo traffic: run red lights, unless there is a policeman at the intersection; never drive with your headlights turned on at night, unless you intend to pass someone or to run a red light; when in doubt or in a hurry, create your own traffic lane, and finally, always, always use your horn instead of your brakes. It is no wonder why many tourists suddenly "get religion" while in Egypt. We gave thanks to the Almighty to have survived the trip to our destination.

The motorcycle touring magazine, Ride, noted in their article, "5 Reasons to Visit Egypt," that if one wanted to experience "the most adventurous thing one can do in Cairo, take a taxi ride through the streets at night." [Ride Magazine, February 2014].

Our beautiful hotel was an exotic vision of salmon pink and gold with delicate waving green palm fronds, splashing water fountains and white stone lions guarding the great double entry doors. It was like walking into an illustration from Aladdin; the building seemed to be edged in gilt, complete with bowing, red fez-wearing servants. In 1869, our hotel had been a palace, built especially for the French Empress Eugenie, when she came to Egypt to open the Suez Canal. Now, that building was the core of the Cairo Marriot Hotel – a thrilling surprise of polished marble floors, sinfully deep sofa cushions, and hanging fretted brass lamps. The lobby seemed to be the crossroads of the world. Three Japanese gentlemen, wearing identical dark business suits, drank tea in a marble arched alcove. A tall, African man, dressed in colorful, flowing robes strode across the lobby, followed by a gaggle of brightly clad women — his wives. German tourists huddled near the Hospitality Desk, working out their next day's itinerary in a loud, animated conversation. In the center of the lobby stood three Gulf State Arabs wearing snow-white robes, and the red and white checkered head coverings which framed their strong, sculpted faces, bristling moustaches, and bright, flashing eyes. They couldn't be for real, I thought. It seemed like I had inadvertently stepped into a movie set from "Lawrence of Arabia," and these handsome men were a young Omar Sharif and his stand-ins, who quietly talked amidst the ebb and flow of the humanity around them. I put down the suitcase that I had been carrying for the past twenty-seven hours across six time zones and stared at the colorful scene around us.

"Yes!" I thought, "Yes, I am really here in Egypt – another world."

The Cairo Marriot Hotel – originally the Gezireh Palace – built in 1869 by the Khedive Ismail for the French Empress Eugenie and other royal guests who came to Egypt for the opening of the Suez Canal. Today, hotel guests are welcomed at the palace's original entrance.

It was a world where Pharaohs once walked, where the Sphinxes asked riddles to wayfarers, where every brass lamp in the local bazaar contained a friendly genie, where the camels were all-wise, but never spoke, where magic could happen at twilight and where dreams had every possibility of coming true.

"Stop staring and close your mouth," my husband whispered to me. "Those Arab guys may get the wrong idea about your morals."

After unpacking our suitcases, washing our faces, and taking short naps in our beautiful hotel room, Marty and I were ready for the official Meet'n'Greet of our Ten Glorious Days tour group at the dinner that was laid out for us in the hotel's lavish Arabian-style billiard room. Our Merry Band of fellow travelers were twelve couples of various ages and stages of life. Together, we represented every corner of the United States.

Two sisters of a certain age had joined up from across the far reaches of the North American Continent to experience Egypt together. Ginger hailed from Southern California in the far West, while her sister Polly had flown in from Connecticut. She represented the New England section of our country. Two couples from Alabama spoke in the soft Southern accents of Dixieland. Griff and her husband Craig accompanied their good friends Vic and Betty. Vic was a newspaper publisher back in Alabama. Bill and Joy had flown all the way from Oregon in the far Pacific Northwest. Bill had been an orthopedist consultant for the Nike Shoe Corporation and, now retired, he was taking his beloved Joy on the trip of her dreams.

Representing the Mid-Western states were two couples from Illinois: Av & Joyce joined their friends, Dale & Harriet. For the next two weeks, these four people stuck together, were game for any experience and they smiled a lot. Marty & I, hailing from Virginia, represented the Middle Atlantic states. The remaining five couples came from all parts of California. Rick & Carol, and Norm & Helen were in Egypt to enjoy ten days of gentle adventures. But George, also from California, had arrived in Egypt triple-strapped with a plethora of photographic equipment that included two hand cameras, a video cam with tripod, and a portable tape recorder for preserving his on-the-spot narrative. His long-suffering wife was Gladys, who spent the next ten days being the object of her husband's nasty mind-games. George was a psychiatrist; Gladys was a saint.

The two "youngsters" of the group were Fred & Mary – a couple of 40-somethings from California who were "doing the Middle East." Following our Ten Glorious Days in Egypt, they planned to go scuba diving in the Red Sea, and then visit Israel for a week. Our Merry Band was completed by a cheerful Californian sportscaster, Vin, and his gorgeous wife Sandi, who was the kindest person on the trip.

Marty, Mohammed & Mary at Kitchener's Gardens. Note Mohammed's gazelle horn cane.

CHAPTER THREE

"FOLLOW THE DANCING GAZELLE HORN!"

"**M**y name is Mohammed," our guide from the Abercrombie and Kent Tour Company introduced himself after breakfast on the first morning of our Glorious Ten Days in Egypt. His deep brown eyes took on an extra twinkle; his sleek, well-groomed moustache twitched. "Mohammed – like everyone else around here."

The twenty-six of us laughed – he had gotten us with that joke! He had also got us, his captive audience, for the next eight days. We followed Mohammed everywhere, often at a trot, over uneven temple floors that were three thousand years old, through crowded bazaars filled with wildly gesturing bead-sellers, into fantastic tombs where thousands of other tourists had gone before. Yes, even into the depths of that rocky moonscape known as the Valley of the Kings at Thebes did we follow Mohammed. In one hand, he cupped an ever-present lighted cigarette. In the other, he clutched his badge of office – a highly polished walking stick that was topped with a real gazelle horn. When we adventurers had lingered too long in one place, just to snap one more photo; when we had turned our attention for just one extra moment to check out the nearest eager seller of scarabs; when we became separated from the rest of our Merry Band, only to discover that we were listening to Interesting Facts of Luxor being presented in rapid-fire French, then we would look to the sky above the throng where Mohammed's gazelle horn waved in excited circles, summoning us back to the tour bus.

Ah, Mohammed! He could read ancient hieroglyphics backwards with the same ease as we Americans can read the Sunday comics in our newspapers. Mohammed spoke of each Pharoah by name as reverently as if that ancient, mummified king was the dearest friend of his. During the next ten days, Mohammed herded the two dozen of us with amazing speed through crowded museums, death-defying traffic, the inscrutable EgyptAir flight schedules, and across narrow two-by-four gangplanks into small, wind-propelled sailboats called feluccas. We followed Mohammed through thick and thin – mostly thick crowds, heavy thick smells of backed-up plumbing and thick smoke in general – while we madly took pictures, took notes, and took in, with greater or lesser degree, the vast amount of Egyptology that our energetic guide imparted to us between the hours of 9 AM and 6 PM daily, Sundays included. In terms of facts-per-minute, we certainly got our money's worth with Mohammed.

And everywhere we looked, there were faces. Egypt seemed to be filled with thousands of faces. Expectant faces begged us for baksheesh [a handout]. Wary faces, calculating faces watched us as we shopped. ["How much should I charge for that souvenir?"] Passersby stared up at us as our air-conditioned tour bus inched its way through the never-ending Cairo traffic. Deep brown eyes followed us at open-air bazaars, hoping to sell us just one more bead necklace. Faces looked over the tall, brass coffee pots as we poured ourselves a second cup of rich coffee.

Other faces surrounded us on our journey through Egypt's epic history – cold stone sneers of long-dead pharaohs; sidelong glances of the naked dancing girls painted on the walls of three-thousand-year-old tombs; impish expressions on tiny statuettes called ushabtis. Everywhere we looked, the faces of Egyptians, past and present, watched us as we tourists moved through their world. Most of all were the faces that abounded in the Egyptian Museum of Antiquities which we visited on our first morning in Cairo.

Built in 1902, the original Egyptian Museum lay deep in central Cairo at Tahrir Square. This rambling, two-level building was the home of over 120,000 items, making it the largest collection of Egyptian artifacts in the world. Every nook and cranny of this enormous museum was crammed with faces from the past. They spanned over five thousand years of history; their kohl-lined eyes were everywhere – watching us as we wandered past them. It was hard to think that behind each face was a name, a person, a story. I felt surrounded, lost in the gaze of history that stared back at me. Motivated by self-preservation, I resolved to find one face – just one in this enormous museum — and get to know that one up close and personal, as they say.

But which face could I choose? Not the famous boy-king Tutankhamun; his story had been done to death, literally. And Nefertiti? Her face had launched a thousand perfume and jewelry advertisements. The heretic pharaoh, Akhenaten? He had a much different face with his elongated chin, thick droopy lips and eyes that were more than a little weird. He looked like the kind of guy with whom I usually tried to avoid sharing an elevator. Or perhaps, he would be the man wearing the sandwich board sign that said something like "Repent! The end of the World is at hand!" No, King Akhenaten was not the face for me.

Princess Nofert in the Museum of Antiquities.

Then, around the corner, I spied the visage that stopped me. There she sat, inside a large, display case. I could tell at first glance that she had been a high-born lady – a three-thousand-year-old classy dame. Now she stared out at the milling crowd of foreigners with a noble bearing. She looked beyond the living faces who pressed against her glass box from all sides. I could tell that she had always known exactly who she was, and no doubt, the real, living woman, now depicted in clay and paint here, would have found it a great indignity to be displayed before such a rabble as us foreign tourists. If ever her spirit – her Ka – returned from the confines of the netherworld, no doubt her painted lips would curl at us with exquisite distain. Looking at the lady inside her box, I could almost hear her thinking, "What am I doing here? And who let in all this riffraff?"

Her statue was dressed carefully in still-bright paint. No doubt she wore the height of Third Dynasty fashion. From the expression on her face, I could tell that she knew she was looking good. Her modern-day counterparts shopped at Harrod's in London, Saks Fifth Avenue in New York, or Rodeo Drive in Los Angeles. She would be the woman, dressed in sleek feline fashion, who would be photographed stepping out of a long, black car as her smiling chauffeur tipped his hat. This ancient Egyptian fashionista wore a white, off-the-shoulder gown which was woven of such sheer linen that her erect, painted nipples jutted proudly, unashamedly, through the fabric. No doubt, she would be thinking, "Look at me, dahlings, but don't you dare touch!"

The Lady's rich necklace was made of six bands of alternating colors and stones – black, green, and red – from which dangled teardrops of gleaming gold. The style was simple, and it was as elegant today as it had been five thousand years ago. She also wore a huge, black wig, perfectly curled and coiffed, which was held in place by a simple headband of white material, embroidered with lotus flowers that were picked out in red and gold. Her own natural hair, black as a raven's wing, peeked out from under the head band. I wondered if she ever got a headache, wearing such a heavy wig. Her eyes were thickly lined in black kohl, but her face, caught forever by the artist, needed no other cosmetics to enhance her proud beauty.

"Who were you?" I wondered.

Then I looked deep into her eyes. Did I detect a hint of fear behind that haughty gaze? Did all that costly finery hide a frightened heart? Was that why she seemed to pull her flimsy shawl so tightly around herself?

Did all her wealth, which she so proudly displayed, not protect her from an overbearing husband? Or did she fear the sidelong glances of her silent slaves, stolen from a dozen nations? Or was it the approach of night, and the steps of her father who came to her bed that caused the tiny tremble on her painted lips?

Times and fashions may have changed down through the ages, but sadly, people and their problems do not. Standing outside her glass case, I felt a tear pricking my eyelids for her, Princess Nofert, beloved of the Gods and daughter of Pharoah. Though she lived in 2720 BC, one could still read the silent plea for help that was in her eyes – a plea that crossed forty centuries. It was a plea that was as desperate then as it is today.

CHAPTER FOUR

HOW OLD IS *OLD*?

Speaking realistically, it is impossible to experience forty centuries of history and culture in Ten Glorious Days, but our packaged tour company gave it their best shot. Our itinerary, which we, so innocently, had chosen six months earlier, had promised they would "show you everything." Now it ran us ragged. Each day was crammed with at least two temples plus one Major Event, like a felucca sailboat ride on the Nile, or the shopping spree in the Khan El Khalili, Cairo's huge open-air bazaar. After a few over-packed days, a lot of Great Sights of Egypt began to run together, despite Mohammed's best efforts to keep us straight along Egypt's long, long historical timeline. Egyptian tour operators live in cold fear that American tourists would not be kept busy enough, so we were on the go from dawn to dusk, being culturally stimulated every split second, lest we complain that "we were robbed!" by our tour company.

Mystery writer and Egyptologist Elizabeth Peters gently mocked her fellow Americans in her thriller, Lion in The Valley: "Show me the pyramid, ma'am. I came a long way to see it and see it I will." A fictional loud American tourist, Mrs. Axhammer of Des Moines, Iowa didn't intend to "do Egypt" by halves. "I've got a list," she said, ". . . and I'm not going home till I've seen everything that's writ down here." She waved a piece of wrinkled paper in heroine Amelia Peabody's face.

So here we are on Glorious Day Three, booted and hatted, slathered in sunscreen lotion, bedecked with cameras, and water bottles, tape recorders and video cams, our pockets stuffed with lots of Egyptian paper money, as well as that most necessary accessory of all — camper's TP. Our Merry Band were ready to be amazed by everything that was "writ down" in our inviolate itineraries. In fact, one could say that our itinerary was written in stone, but it was the little things, the unexpected surprises, that linger the brightest in my memories.

At Saqqara in Memphis, outside of Cairo, we were as far out in the Western Desert as we were ever going to get. . . in this life, at least. The cultivated fields of banana trees and clover fields were now out of sight behind a high, rocky escarpment. Despite the brilliant sun, there was a surprising chill wind that blew out of the endless wasteland to the west, as we trooped obediently behind Mohammed and his gazelle horn walking stick to our first Temple of the Day – the Step Pyramid of Zoser [Third Dynasty, 2670 – 2650 BC]. This monument was okay, though it reminded me of the squashy birthday cake I once made when I was doing the Girl Scout Cooking Badge – a little saggy and rough around the edges with extra "frosting" [loose rocks] sliding to the bottom. Since this was our first bona fide pyramid of the tour, our traveling companions snapped photos like crazy. George untied his tripod, strapped on his video cam and the tape recorder simultaneously, then spent at least fifteen minutes narrating what he could remember about the Step Pyramid for the edification of "the folks back home in California." His patient wife, Gladys quietly wandered away and enjoyed the beauty of the desert on her own.

Carpeting the rocky hard-packed ground were thousands of small, reddish pebbles. They were the most unusual-looking stones that I had ever seen. They didn't look like they were natural rocks, since the surrounding ground was a sandy brown color as far as the eye could see. I picked up a few then located Mohammed, our university graduate guide, who was smoking a cigarette next to our tour bus. He looked closely at the bits in my hand.

"Pottery shards," he informed me. Was he serious? Here, in the middle of nowhere?

"How old?" I asked.

"Ver-ry old," he replied solemnly, rolling his "r"s.

"Old as in . . ." I waved at an ancient tomb opening nearby. I was afraid to ask for a specific dating. I wanted to enjoy my moment of amateur archeology.

Mohammed nodded gravely. "Ver-ry old," he repeated. "You can take them. You keep them."

I was afraid to breathe. A pottery fragment, the size of an American quarter, looked more like a dusty red nugget top and bottom. Sandwiched in the middle was the now-familiar gray of Nile clay like we had seen in pottery funeral dishes in the Museum of Antiquities. The sides of my fragment were worn; a few grains of sand lodged in a crack. On the top was the faint indentation of a fingerprint. Was I really holding a piece of ancient history in my hand?

Here at Saqqara in the Western Desert, there were no violent desert storms ever, no rain for centuries, no disturbance except for tourists' feet walking over the thick carpet of pottery shards. For whose funeral was this clay dish or offering bowl smashed by grieving relatives? What offerings to the dead did it contain? Who had made it? The potter had fashioned probably a hundred of these reddish clay containers every day. It was literally a throw-away, no artwork necessary – just like the paper cups that we use today, and then toss into the trash. And here I was, maybe hundreds of centuries later, holding a bit of an ancient bowl in my hand. I felt like an archeologist, like the fictional Amelia Peabody or maybe the movie hero, Indiana Jones. In that moment, Egyptian history was more alive in the palm of my hand than ever in the grand edifice of the Zoser pyramid, rising behind me.

Visiting the Zoser Step Pyramid. Note the "pebbles on the ground" – they are thousands of ancient pottery shards.

Then the gazelle horn waved in the air. "Everyone back in the bus, please. We have many places still to visit. But first, luncheon at Giza."

It was not just any old lunch at a hot dog stand. Our bus pulled up beside the world-famous Mena House Hotel on the Giza Plateau. The Mena House had been constructed in 1869 as part of the run-up to the opening of the Suez Canal. The Khedive Ismail had built it only a stone's throw from Giza's famous Pyramids as a gateway and rest house for his famous guests who would be visiting Egypt for the canal's opening. In later years, Mena House was turned into a hotel for the rich and famous, and it is now part of the Marriot hotel chain, offering 5-star amenities. When our bus pulled into the Hotel's driveway, we came to a sudden stop. Something interesting was happening at the hotel's main entrance. Mohammed quickly ushered us off the bus and told us to stand still, be quiet and no photographing, please.

I knew that George's fingers just itched for his cameras.

Under the portico in front of the hotel, a gorgeous oriental rug was spread out on the asphalt, and a half-dozen beautifully adorned horses danced back and forth on it to the music of drums, flutes, and cymbals. A Saudi Prince, wearing full Arabian regalia, including an ornamental dagger at his belt, had arrived to stay at this hotel, and he was being accorded the honor of a traditional Bedouin welcome as befitted his noble birth. The horses' golden trappings, red tassels, and dangling brass bells swayed in time with the rhythm of the music. I knew, without sneaking a look, that George was dying to photograph this moment, but Mohammed's glare stopped him from provoking an international incident.

Then suddenly, the music ceased, and the welcome fanfare was over. Horses, musicians, the carpet, and the prince all disappeared in several directions at once. No applause please, our nervous guide cautioned. Then we moved inside the Mena House, in awed silence, to enjoy a delicious lunch. An hour and a half later, our Merry Band was back on the bus, and we chugged up a low rise toward the Seventh Wonder of the World.

I first became aware of the land of Egypt at the tender age of five. At that time, my mother was a two-pack-a-day smoker, and her brand of choice was Camel cigarettes. I was fascinated by the picture on the front of those packs, amazed by the camel, the pyramids, and the palm trees – three things I had never seen for real in my short life. In the imperious manner of a spoiled and dearly beloved grandchild, I demanded my grandparents to take me immediately to the Land of Camel Cigarettes. The best that my ever-patient grandfather could do at the time was to take me to the zoo and show me their specimen of a camel.

Alas! Huge disappointment! The zoo's only camel was a Bactrian, which had two humps, not one. No matter what my grandfather said, I knew that the zoo's two-humped species was not a "real camel." It was years before I recovered from that childhood trauma. Only when I was in college in San Diego, California did I finally see the true single-humped Arabian camel, also known by his friends as a "dromedary." The world-famous San

Diego Zoo justly enjoys its renowned reputation. It had not only both types of camels on display, but it even had real palm trees growing out of the ground, instead of out of large brass pots. But, alas, there were no pyramids in San Diego. I had to wait another twenty-seven years before finally seeing the whole living picture depicted on the cigarette pack.

After our delicious lunch on the afternoon of Day Two, our plucky little band boarded the tour bus and ten minutes later we arrived on the Giza Plateau – home of camels, pyramids, and date palms. I was excited. I was prepared to be amazed. I had waited all my life for this moment, and there they were before me – the Pyramids, the greatest building project ever constructed by mankind.

I tried to be impressed. My fellow travelers were all excited and snapping pictures through the bus's dingy windows. Yes, there they were the pyramids, looking exactly like every picture in every book on Egypt that I found in the Fairfax, Virginia's Public Library. Seen at first in the distance, they appeared low and squat and a little fuzzy around the edges. They did not look big; I was expecting big – like the Washington Monument in my hometown of Washington, DC. That was big.

Meanwhile, all my fellow travelers were thrilled to be so near to the world's most famous buildings. The Merry Band snapped pictures and spoke in high-pitched exclamation points.

"It will get better when we get closer to them," I told myself. After all, Julius Caesar loved the pyramids. Alexander the Great adored them. Napoleon Bonaparte even slept in one. Millions of people for thousands of years couldn't have been wrong about these majestic buildings. Surely, it was me – I must be missing the point.

As our bus drew nearer to the parking lot, the pyramids did get bigger, but not much better in my eyes. Maybe I was jaded; I was too used to the skyscrapers back in the States, I reasoned. Meanwhile, the picture-taking around me had reached epic proportions. I pretended to be excited. Our tour bus came to a rattling stop beside the Great Pyramid of Cheops.

"Now," I said to myself, as we shuffled off the bus, and advanced toward the base of the largest one. "Now I will feel the thrill of excitement and the joy I have dreamed about for so many years." But I didn't. Instead, Mark Twain's observation of the pyramids, written in 1867, came to mind.

"I could conjure up no comparison that would convey to my mind a satisfactory comprehension of the magnitude of a pile of monstrous stones that covered thirteen acres of ground and stretched upward four hundred and eighty tiresome feet, so I gave it up," he wrote.

I did try to appreciate this pyramid – I really did. I craned my neck and looked up; but all I could see was a wall of rough-cut stone. The shape and scope of this building was literally out of sight, angling away toward the blue heavens. I ran my hand along one of the great blocks that formed the bottom tier, and I tried to imagine the man who had worked on this very stone four thousand years ago. I closed my eyes as I traced the rough square and listened with my inner ear to hear ancient chisels striking the granite, and to taste the grit of the powdery dust. I listened for the sound of the off-key song of the stone cutter was he worked. I tried to envision his sweat and his tears, and even his bloody hands that had pushed this huge rock into its everlasting position. But I felt nothing.

On the other hand, my husband was ecstatic. "Okay, Schaller," he said to me. "Let's go!"

"Go where?" I asked, looking at the wall of rock in front of me.

"Inside!"

"Inside . . . that?" I pointed to the enormous rock pile. I suffer from a mild case of claustrophobia, and Marty knew it.

"If you don't go up inside there, you will always regret it," he warned. "This is your one and only chance to get up close and personal with a pyramid. We are not coming back here ever again."

With that, he turned away and started walking toward a large hole in one side of the base. "It's now or never!" was his parting shot over his shoulder.

I scampered quickly after him. If I was going to get lost, entombed, and suffocated in the darkness with a thousand writhing snakes coiling themselves companionably around me, at least I would die in my husband's arms. I had seen an awful lot of Indiana Jones movies.

For the first fifteen or twenty feet inside the Seventh Wonder, we were able to walk upright and in a straight line. Then the going got nasty. My claustrophobia is nothing compared to my fear of heights. I grow ridged, dizzy, and clammy all at the same time when confronted with any-thing higher than the diving springboard at our neighborhood swimming pool. Now, inside this hellhole, a narrow three-foot wide shaft opened – the Grand Gallery – with a flaking, yellow-painted wooden ladder going up the long, dimly-lit slope. Without a backward glance of support, Marty crouched down and started crawling up the rungs, hand over hand, into the dark recesses of the Twelfth of Never that was only faintly lit by occasional naked light bulbs. Behind me, several other members of our Merry Band waited and waited while I swallowed down my thumping heart, grabbed a wooden slat of the ladder, and followed up after the man, whose neck I most wanted to wring at that moment.

"What this puppy needs is an escalator," panted Joyce from Chicago, who was climbing right behind me. At this point, we were hanging onto the ladder at a thirty-degree angle and about sixty feet up inside this royal tomb with no end in sight beyond the feeble light bulb ahead.

I nodded, wiping the perspiration out of my eyes, and praying that the dim lights above us would not suddenly go out. I touched the small flashlight inside my pants' pocket for good luck.

"There is no end to this climb," I thought to myself, when we were somewhere around a hundred feet nearly straight up. Considering the crowd climbing behind me, going back down was not an option. We continued to crawl precariously up the shaft. The beauty of its ancient engineering was completely lost on me as I hung onto the ladder and did not allow myself to look down.

"We are going to be in here forever," I muttered aloud to myself.

"You know what?" asked Joyce in a cheerful voice behind me, "Isn't this about the spot where the boulder rolls down the passageway in *Raiders of The Lost Ark*?"

I nodded, swallowed, and looked up. My husband's form was now almost beyond the available light source. Joyce was right; we were doomed. If only I had a trusty bullwhip now – except there wasn't enough room in this upward tunnel to swing a cat, let alone a bullwhip. I nodded again, and briefly wondered if I had told our children where our Last Wills were located. What was I doing here, hanging onto a rickety ladder somewhere between heaven and hell?

"Nearly there!" Marty's voice echoed off the walls ahead of me. I could barely see him, much less any escape hatch.

At one-hundred-and-fifty-three feet above the earth, we finally arrived on a stone platform at the top of the shaft, only to be confronted by an enormous granite slab, twenty inches thick, that hung two-thirds of the way down the only doorway. Technically, it was called a "portcullis stone," meaning "gate," and it appeared that nothing, but the grace of the Almighty, was holding it three feet above the stone floor. I could swear that I heard an ominous "creak" as I slithered on all fours underneath it.

At least, we could now stand up inside the King's Burial Chamber, which was empty except for several dozen other hardy tourists, and a large open granite sarcophagus in one corner. The roof – all forty tons of it – arched high over our heads without any visible rafters. The air inside the chamber was heavy with humidity, heat, steaming bodies – and the smell of stale urine. It reminded me of the ladies' locker room at our local swimming pool on a blistering hot summer day. As we drew nearer to the sarcophagus, I realized where the smell was coming from. Some uncivilized tourists liked to carve their names into ancient walls, while others liked to pee into ancient coffins.

The return trip down the ladder was again like a scene out of Indiana Jones. This time, I rolled quickly under the hanging portcullis stone, just like Harrison Ford had done in "*Raiders.*" As an actor, Mr. Ford only had to roll under a painted plaster and wire slab, while we crazy tourists in Egypt were rolling under twenty tons of free-hanging granite. Going backwards down the ladder behind Marty seemed a lot easier on the return trip as he talked me down the rungs. As we neared the bottom of the shaft, I felt the cooler air. At last, standing safely outside the Great Pyramid, savoring our escape from certain death, I shelved my memory of this Ultimate Experience. Three years later, in 1995, the Egyptian government made this adventure a lot tamer. Nowadays, tourists climb a long permanent stone staircase of the Grand Gallery shaft to the Burial Chamber. There is also a permanent handrail attached to the wall on which to cling every step of the way. In retrospect, I am a little sorry for the modernization. Now that I am safely back on level ground, I can admit that I had relished my brief, but hair-raising Indiana Jones experience on that rickety ladder.

Returning to 1992, once Marty and I were safely back outside the pyramid among the living and standing on the packed sand of the Giza plateau, it was time for our Merry Band to move on and meet the camels!

CHAPTER FIVE

"GET A LIFT WITH A CAMEL"

Camels! You either love them or loathe them; there isn't much in between. Camels are not likable. They are smelly, bad-tempered and they tend to spit or bite. They would not look cute and cuddly, folded up in front of your fireplace. I doubt you could paper-train one. Camels seem to dislike people, particularly tourists. One cannot blame them. Tourists act positively stupid around camels. And if there is one thing that can be said in the camel's favor – he isn't stupid. He is crafty.

Personally, I love camels. The French explorer and author Gustave Flaubert adored them, so I am in good company. It had been a life-time ambition of mine to ride upon a camel's back – and not just on any old zoo camel, but one who lived next to the Pyramids in Egypt. It was that early cigarette ad influence. This experience was my only request to Mohammed at the beginning of our Ten Glorious Days, when he had asked us if there was anything special that we wanted to see or do. Other members of our Tour Group were less than enthusiastic to have an up-close-and-personal ride on a camel. Most of them put sitting astride a camel right up there next to oral surgery. On the other hand, everyone was extremely interested in watching Marty and me ride a camel. It would provide great photo ops as well as enter-tainment for our Merry Band.

Mohammed introduced us to another one of his many nationwide cousins, Abdullah. Abdullah happened to have one of the rent-a-camel concessions in the shadow of the Pyramids. Abdullah introduced Marty and me to Fatima. Fatima was a fully-grown camel. Not just any camel, but a real camel who lived by the pyramids and who had a soft, velvet nose, and a richly adorned saddle with swaying red tassels. Fatima possessed a pair of deep "come hither" brown eyes and double eyelashes that I would kill to have. She regarded us with a proud, disdainful glare, and she gave a deep grunt of displeasure when we were loaded onto her back.

I didn't blame her attitude one bit. After all, it was late afternoon, and nearly quitting time. She had endured her share of camera-toting idiots on her back all day long. She had to hear people screeching into her ears in a dozen languages that were not Arabic. She had been looking forward to burying her nose into her large pile of fresh green clover, followed by a good night's sleep. Fatima particularly did not want to go out one more time to the Pyramids. I swear I saw a sneaky gleam come into her eyes as she tilted forward, then backward to stand up proudly erect on all her finery.

"Here," said Abdullah, handing Fatima's single rein to me as I was seated in the forward position of our tandem camel saddle. "You hold her."

Mary & Marty aboard Fatima with Abdulla,
just before he handed Fatima's rein to Mary.

Then the little camel driver scurried away to help Joyce and her husband Av as well as Ginger and Polly to get astride on their camels. The rest of our Merry Band, including Mohammed with his ever-present cigarette, watched from inside the safety of the tour bus. They were armed and ready with their cameras. Throwing his caution to the desert breezes, George set up his tripod beside the bus's bumper. Meanwhile our three camels were now standing upright and in position. The stage for revolt had been set. Fatima was ready. Marty and I were not.

The camel driver turned his back.

Slowly, Fatima swung her long graceful neck toward the west, where the sun was heading down. Before we realized what was happening, she had settled into a comfortable lope and was heading across the Great Western Desert. Next stop, Libya! Not that Fatima had considered going the whole two-thousand-mile route through the desert to that country. Her plan was to drop us off somewhere along the way, preferably in the Middle of Nowhere.

"Hey!" exclaimed my husband, clutching me around the waist. Being raised with a stamp collection, he was not used to riding live animals, particularly a camel. "Hey! How do you stop this thing?"

Now I can stop a horse. I can stop goldfish from going down the garbage disposal when I'm changing their water. Stop pet gerbils from escaping their cage. Stop a car at a traffic light, and even bring a roomful of excitable drama students to a full silent standstill. But I had never stopped a camel. I didn't know the word stop in Arabic. "The rein was working.

The Pyramids grew smaller behind us. Abdullah still had his back to us, probably arguing with Mohammad about the price to be paid for the pleasure of our company. The Great Western Desert was getting greater by the minute. I could almost hear Fatima humming a little tune under her breath as she continued to lope toward the setting sun.

"Well, do something!" hissed my husband in my ear. "You've got the reins. You know how to ride a horse, and you're the one who's got her feet in the stirrups."

The hard-packed ground was a good seven or eight feet below us. Adult camels are very tall. I considered jumping off, but it really was a long way down. Besides, that would be admitting defeat to Fatima. Instead, I laid the single rein across her neck and gently tugged. The rein was attached to a red leather collar midway around her neck, and I didn't want to hurt her.

Happily, she started to swing in a wide circle. More to the point, she was swinging back in the direction from whence we had come. The Pyramids rose again in our view. So did the sight of the rotund Abdullah, who had finally noticed that we were missing. Now he was bouncing after us. As we headed back toward our tour group, and Fatima's glistening pile of green clover, the Merry Band, now standing outside the bus, sent up a cheer. Abdullah grasped Fatima's rein as Marty and I smiled and waved to our fellow travelers, who were taking lots of pictures. Our impromptu desert ride was preserved on dozens of rolls of film forever. Marty expressed his joy and relief by squeezing me tightly and waving to the crowd. I grinned. Fatima sighed like a good sport. At least, in her mind, it had been fun while it lasted.

Now that Abdullah had us firmly in hand, he led our camel plus the two others, in a slow procession back to the Pyramids, while our tour bus chugged a safe distance behind us. Strains of the sweeping theme music from the movie *Lawrence of Arabia* filled my imagination as we loped over the ancient sands to the pyramid's parking lot. Fatima's head remained proudly erect. She was nothing if not a good loser, besides her instinct must have told her that she was the focus of a dozen cameras. Her ears were perked and straight. The Pyramids, floating in the lavender haze of the early evening twilight, seem to shimmer as if in a dreamscape.

Oh, yes! Yes! This was more like it. This was the moment that I had first dreamed about so many years ago. It was exactly what I had hoped it would be. We were here, in the legendary land of the pharaohs. The Pyramids rose before us. Any moment now, Peter O'Toole would come riding out of the purple dusk, and invite us to join him in his march to Aqaba, Jordan! Amid the tinkling of small brass bells, Omar Shariff would appear beside us, astride his favorite camel. We were ready for adventure – at least, I was ready. I was not too sure about Marty or Fatima.

Desert sands, gentle camel bells, purple-pink twilight, dreamy Pyramids – and twenty-four fellow travelers snapping yet more pictures of us as fast as their automatic cameras would allow. Now, years later, Marty and I are the proud owners of a large photo album, recording almost every moment we had spent astride the Lady Fatima.

Alas, all good things must come to an end, even a Dream that has come true. Just before boarding our bus that would whisk us away to our final stop of the day, the Papyrus Factory, I turned around for one last look. Abdullah had taken off Fatima's saddle. She stood alone in solitary dignity, allowing the cool evening breeze blowing off the desert to dry the sweat from her back. Behind her, the three Pyramids nestled comfortably together for the night. Just at the edge of my vision, I caught a glimpse of two date palm trees, their fronds waving goodbye in the gentle breeze.

It had taken forty-five years, and a trip of nine thousand miles, but the wait was worth it – camels, pyramids, and palm trees, in that order – just like the picture on the cigarette package.

Marty and Mary's triumphal return aboard Fatima. Behind us is the beginning of the Great Western Desert where Fatima took us on a side trip to Nowhere.

CHAPTER SIX

FLYING THE FRIENDLY SKIES

For Western-born tourists, Americans in particular, the scariest words in the Arabic language are "inshallah mumkin bukra" which means "if God wills it, perhaps tomorrow."

"It will rain tomorrow, perhaps tomorrow." [Note: it hardly ever rains in Egypt.]

"The golden cartouche necklace that you ordered will be ready, if God wills it, perhaps tomorrow."

"I will get that information for you, if God wills it, perhaps tomorrow."

"The EgyptAir flight to Aswan will leave at six-thirty, if God wills it, perhaps tomorrow."

Considering the current state of the world at large, the Good Lord has a lot of other crises on His mind, so EgyptAir is low on His list of priorities. The Good Lord leaves the details of EgyptAir's schedules in the hands of the Egyptians. With a little bit of luck, insha'allah mumkin bukra, the Good Lord will make sure that the airplanes don't fall out of the sky too often. Herein is where problems arise which tend to lead to a great deal of misunderstanding between EgyptAir and the clock-watching citizens of the Western world.

EgyptAir is a fact of life in Egypt. Sooner or later, nearly every visitor gets entangled in the tenacles of its organization – or lack thereof. The most important things for the visitor to do when flying the friendly skies of EgyptAir are to be patient and to maintain a sense of humor.

"Not to worry, lady! Your luggage will be coming, insha'allah mumkin bukra."

EgyptAir is the domestic airline whereby the trusting tourist is whisked from Cairo upstream to Aswan, to Abu Simbel, and then to Luxor – hopefully, not all on the same day. The airplanes themselves are clean, comfortable, and usually air-conditioned. Aboard each aircraft, near the forward door, is a small, beautifully bound copy of the Koran, the Moslem holy book, encased in Plexiglas. Its blue and gold embossed leather cover glistens in the deserts bright sunlight. In ... of ... emergency, does one break the glass?

The cabin crew are attentive and offer canned fruit drinks, even if the flight is only twenty minutes long, as it is when flying from Aswan to Abu Simbel. It is what happens on the ground before and after the flight that will cause a grown Texan to weep.

Nothing happens for long, long unexplained periods of time. Time and EgyptAir are diametrically opposed ideas. The first thing one must get used to are the airports themselves. Whether it is the bustling Cairo International or the Quonset hut which served Abu Simbel in 1992, all the airports in Egypt are military bases, surrounded by barbed wire and guarded by a large number of young soldiers who are bristling with military assault rifles. A soldier with an automatic weapon slung casually over his shoulder was my first sight in Egypt when we got off our airplane in Cairo after travelling twenty-seven hours from Washington, DC. That sight alone was enough to wake me up to full alert.

Three days later, our Merry Band of travelers was scheduled to fly upriver from Cairo to Aswan, five hundred miles in the hot, dry desert to the south. There we would pick up our Nile cruise boat for our Five

Glorious Days of sailing on the Nile, Mother of Rivers. We all beamed with delight. The cruise was what we had been waiting to experience. Then Mohammed informed us that we would be flying out of Cairo at six-thirty the following morning, because the earlier start we got on EgyptAir, the closer we would be to our tour schedule. Our Merry Band tried to look enthusiastic. It was obvious that none of us were crack-of-dawn people, except for my husband who is an early bird out of habit. Many of our fellow travelers were still jet-lagged, having flown from California to Egypt. Then Mohammed said that in order to get to our plane on time, our bus would pick us up at the hotel at five-thirty in the morning. We rolled our collective eyes and tried to look excited. Therefore, Mohammed continued, our wake-up call would be at four-thirty in the middle of the night.

"This will be a new experience for you," Marty purred into my ear. At home, he jogs every morning at the crack of dawn. "You will discover that there is life before breakfast."

I was not amused.

The following morning at 5 am, our sleepy Merry Band discovered that there was a great deal of life going on in the Cairo Marriot Hotel at that ungodly hour. The disco and casino were both still open and in full swing. An all-night wedding party was still going strong as we intrepid travelers groped our way to the near-empty Omar Khayyam Restaurant for breakfast. Down the hallway, gyrating music with a strong percussion beat accompanied our meal of corn flakes and coffee. Then, in the darkest hour before the dawn, we loaded up our suitcases and shopping bags into the tour bus, and, with Cairo's morning rush hour horns blaring, we headed into the clutches of EgyptAir.

As much, much later events proved, Mohammed was right. We did fly out of Cairo on time – only forty-five minutes late, which was practically a record for promptness.

Though we had been encouraged to take photographs at every possible moment of our Ten Glorious Days in Egypt, we quickly learned that picture-taking in any airport or surrounding area was strictly prohibited. We were warned that, at the very least, our film would be confiscated and destroyed. Mohammed did not tell us what would happen in the worst-case scenario. It was not a comforting thought, especially so early in the morning. Looking at the soldiers who surrounded the tarmac, it quickly became apparent to us that these guys meant business – presuming, of course, that their rifles were really loaded. Not even George, with all his photographic equipment dangling off both shoulders, attempted to snap a forbidden picture.

An hour or so later we landed at the Aswan airport, now bathed in the bright mid-morning's sunlight. Then we sat in our seats and waited for the permission to get off the plane. Looking out our cabin's tiny window, we saw a lone guard standing near the runway, and staring out at the sand dunes of the Nubian Desert which surrounded the airport. Perhaps he was there to assure our safety as we stepped down the rickety, rolling staircase to board the airport's single minivan. We had lots of opportunity to observe this guard – who happened to be young and good-looking – as we waited for the anticipated rolling stairway to inch its way down the runway to our plane, and for the arrival of the promised minivan, that was nowhere in sight. There was absolutely nothing to look at through our cabin window except barbwire fencing, a lot of sand and our lone guard.

This handsome young protector carried his gun over his shoulder in a raffish manner. He clutched his ammunition clip in one hand, and his cigarette pack in the other. He was either a rapid chain-smoker or else very nervous. We wondered, among ourselves, if there were armed bandits lurking behind the sand dunes.

Watching him, the question arose in my mind, what would happen in an actual emergency? If the guard was nervous now, what would happen if a group of desperados really did swarm over the barbed wire fence? Would our protector try to jam a cigarette into his gun while attempting to smoke a bullet?

Just then, our airplane's intercom burst into sudden life. "The passenger bus will be here in a moment, insha'allah mumkin."

We craned our necks as everyone tried to peer out our windows. Yes? Where was the promised van? At least, the slow rolling stairway had finally lurched to a stop in front of the plane's open door. Yet, still we waited, buckled snugly in our seats. The distance between our plane and the terminal looked to be about a quarter mile long. Most of us could have walked it easily. However, we were on a military base, and tourists were not permitted into unauthorized areas. Presumably, this rule included the asphalt between us and the terminal's door. Finally, Allah smiled down upon us sweating inside the stifling plane, and the airport's only van arrived.

Once inside the empty terminal, the overhead speakers squawked to life. "Passengers, please remain in the Baggage Claim Area until your baggage has arrived, insha'allah mumkin."

So again, we waited, this time in the dry, hot baggage claim area while the airport van crept back out to our plane. Our less-than-Merry Band waited and watched as the driver of the van met the single baggage handler at the door of our airplane's hold. We waited and watched while the two men in charge of all our goods and chattels shook hands, smoked several cigarettes, and began a long and animated conversation, accompanied by flying cigarette ashes. We waited and watched as slowly, one by one, our battered bags emerged into the now-baking sunlight. Then, one by one, they were flung into the van. We watched and waited, less patiently than before, as the two custodians of our worldly possessions smoked final cigarettes, shook hands again and parted. Our tour group, with our noses pressed against the dirty glass windows, murmured a collective sigh of relief.

But not yet.

Upon the arrival of the baggage at the terminal, and within plain sight of all of us, there was yet another round of handshaking, cigarette smoking and conversation between the van driver and the airport's only luggage handler before even one suitcase was lifted onto the conveyer belt.

"Patience, patience," Marty murmured in my ear. "Our suitcases will be here soon, and we will be on our way."

"Insha'allah mumkin," I replied, barely moving my dry lips. A nearby Egyptian, recognizing his native tongue and favorite phrase being savaged by a foreign accent, turned toward us, smiled broadly, and waved.

It was eleven o'clock in the morning by the time the twenty-six of us, carrying all our worldly belongings, fell out of the airport van and staggered aboard our Nile cruiser, the Sun Boat, that was docked at the Aswan town pier. We were greeted by the boat manager with cold, refreshing glasses of red hibiscus juice, which tasted like the nectar of the gods.

However, our adventure with EgyptAir was not yet over. Four hours later, after a delicious lunch and a refreshing nap aboard the Sun Boat, we found ourselves back at the Aswan Airport for the "short" flight over Lake Nassar to visit what is one of the finest of the ancient Egyptian monuments, Abu Simbel. We were promised that it would be only a twenty-minute flight down the lake, then two leisurely hours to visit both temples there, before our half-hour flight back to Aswan and dinner aboard our Nile cruiser at six-thirty. No problem, insha'allah mumkin. Except – there was no plane waiting for us on the runway at three PM. An hour later, the plane had not yet arrived. Mohammed, our intrepid tour guide, dozed in the waiting lounge. The smiling soldiers, baggage handlers, ticket personnel and janitors all looked unconcerned by the delay. We Americans shifted positions in our plastic seats and stared out the streaky windows. As before, there was only the empty runway, the barbed wire fence and a sea of rolling sand dunes that stretched to the horizon.

What could be happening to our plane? I wondered. Was it out of gas? Was there only one plane that went back and forth to Abu Simbel? Had it gotten lost somewhere over the vast desert wastes with a load of brave passengers, who, at this very moment, were making a Gerry-rigged wind-rider out of a broken wing and parachute silk? Or, horror of horrors, was that load of brave, patient travelers still waiting at the Abu Simbel air strip, and wondering what was holding us up?

Suddenly, out of the bright blue sky, a plane landed. We forced ourselves not to cheer. Mohammed roused himself from his afternoon nap. We leapt to our collective feet with giddy anticipation. Then Mohammed held up a warning hand. No, this was not our plane. This one had just arrived from Cairo, five hundred miles to the north. Our now less-than-Merry Band collapsed back in our uncomfortable plastic chairs and watched, with grim enjoyment, while this planeload of these new, unsuspecting tourists spent an incredible amount of time waiting for their luggage to be off-loaded.

Waiting.

Look! Up in the sky! Is it a bird? Is it a plane? Is it our plane, we dared to hope? Some of us mumbled a quick prayer. At least, some of us were mumbling something under their breathes. I make it a point of honor never to eavesdrop on other people's devotions. Just then, Mohammed roused himself again. We sat up straighter in our chairs with expectation. Mohammed stood up; we stood up. Mohammed smiled under his black moustache. We stampeded for the door. It was now almost five o'clock in the afternoon. At this point, we had been traveling to Abu Simbel for almost twelve hours.

The long wait was worth it. Abu Simbel is the most awesome temple in Egypt – awesome for the sheer size of the four colossi statues of Rameses the Great which flank the entrance, and awesome for the fact that this whole thing, mountain included, was moved five miles upriver and placed on a cliff ninety feet above Lake Nasser's rising waters by UNESCO during the 1960s. However, some of our Merry Band, even amid such a magnificent place, were grumbling. Because we had arrived so late in the afternoon, the February twilight was already creeping upon us. This prompted everyone to start taking pictures like crazed paparazzi from People Magazine before the light faded away. In the deepening twilight, the lake below us turned the color of purple ink, while the sky crept into violet hues. Then, suddenly, when no one expected it, the entire facade of Abu Simbel was lit up by the powerful beams of electric lights. The gigantic statues appeared to come alive; one could almost see them breathing. Did we hear a soft sigh escape from those stone lips? Did we detect the flutter of a stone eyelash? Like a colony of worker ants, we scurried between the ponderous legs of the ancient Pharoah, casting nervous glances at those huge feet, lest they move and squash us. The temple's inner sanctum was awash in a golden glow. Egypt wove her magic spell upon all of us.

Abu Simbel had been constructed as the gateway to Upper Egypt from the southern countries of Nubia and the Sudan. This temple was meant to be the ultimate Customs and Immigration checkpoint for ancient travelers coming up from Africa's interior. Just imagine the faces of those African traders, paddling their dugout boats, when they rounded the upper bend of the Nile and saw those huge images of the god-man Pharoah waiting for them. "Abandon hope all ye who enter here!" Abu Simbel, by the purple twilight, was incredibly powerful, and, in retrospect, I wouldn't have wanted to visit it at any other time of day. There was just one little fly in the in the ointment of our pleasure. We still had to go back to Aswan and the Sun Boat by way of EgyptAir.

It was pitch black outside at 6 pm when we returned to the tiny Abu Simbel terminal and settled ourselves on those uncomfortable plastic chairs while we waited for the plane to take us back to Aswan. By now, we were quiet. Some of us were meditating upon the stirring sights we had just photographed and video-taped for posterity. Many of us experienced a groggy déjà vu. Wasn't this the very same place that we had arrived at hours ago? Some of us were dreaming of the promised dinner waiting for us aboard the good ship Sun Boat. Some of us were reading our guidebooks.

None of us expected the mouse.

Abu Simbel is in the middle of Nowhere. The airport is even more removed from the monuments at Abu Simbel. Meanwhile, the desert night filled with thousands of beady little eyes, most of them belonging to a species of Egypt's desert rodent known as a jerboa, who are first cousins of the common pet store gerbil. This five-inch-long mouse had made a wrong turn and it wound up in the middle of a waiting room filled with tired, hungry American tourists, half of whom were female.

Shrieks! Screams! Leaping onto wobbly plastic chairs! In short, it was a little diversion to while away the time until EgyptAir decided to retrieve us. On the other hand, this bit of excitement was just what the armed-and-ready Egyptian state militia wanted. Rushing boldly to the defense of Womanhood, one of the guards affixed a shiny bayonet to his rifle, gave chase to the squeaking intruder and . . .

(No, I am not making this up.)

. . . nailed it literally dead in the middle of the floor. One of our ladies dashed to the restroom. Several others gagged as the proud National Guardsman exited the room, holding aloft his fresh, bleeding trophy on the end of his bayonet.

I felt very sorry for the jerboa.

Fortunately, the last plane to Aswan arrived at that exact moment.

Our first dinner aboard the Sun Boat was served at eight-thirty that evening. By that time, our Merry Band had been awake for sixteen hours.

Five days later, after we had expressed a heartfelt farewell to the Sun Boat Manager and his charming crew, we were hurled once again onto the tender mercies of EgyptAir at the Luxor Airport for our flight back to Cairo. Luxor has an international airport since many airlines from other parts of the world bypass Cairo and fly directly to Luxor, which was once the capital city of ancient Egypt. Consequently, the Luxor airport security was much tighter than expected.

By this time, on our Ninth Glorious Day in Egypt, I had purchased almost everything on our lengthy, pre-trip shopping list, including a water-pipe for our new son-in-law. I was especially pleased with this purchase not only because it looked like the one that the Blue Caterpillar smoked in Alice in Wonderland, but also because I could take it apart in five easy pieces for packing. Naturally, I had wrapped each piece and padded it carefully with my increasing supply of used laundry.

The whole thing looked like a bomb when my carry-on bag went through the Luxor Airport security x-ray. A little red light started flashing on the machine. Two armed soldiers descended upon me; their Uzis unhitched from their shoulders. Naturally, Marty had chosen this exact time to use the Gents' restroom.

I unzipped my over-stuffed bag. A brownish sock that had been fluffy white last week fell out, followed by a pair of my unmentionables. A third soldier arrived on the scene. Marty was still in the Gents. I began unwrapping the first piece of the hubbly-bubbly that was on top – the brass mid-section which was the pipe part.

"It's a water pipe," I explained. My lips were very dry and felt numb.

"Open, please," said the third guard, repeating the total of his English vocabulary.

"Hubbly-bubbly!" I made puffing motions. The guards closed in around me. Marty was taking a very long time in the Gents.

"Hookah!" I cried in desperation, remembering that word from my reading of A Thousand and One Arabian Nights.

The guards relaxed and stepped back. Everyone smiled at me. The first guard shook my hand. The third guard sighed as my Victoria Secret undies disappeared back into my bag. Then the young men waved me through Security. My knees felt locked in position.

"What kept you?" Marty asked as I fell into the chair beside him in the waiting lounge. I decided not to stir up husbandly outrage against the

Egyptian Security. One international confrontation a day was about all I could handle at my age.

"I had to re-pack the waterpipe," I said with a sigh.

"I knew that we'd never get that damned thing home in one piece," he muttered.

"Insha'allah mumkin bukra." I closed my eyes for a little nap. The EgyptAir plane to Cairo was predictably two hours late.

One of the beautiful columns of the Greco-Roman temple of Philae,
dedicated to the Egyptian goddess Isis. Built approximately 690 BC,
it is one of the newest ancient Egyptian temples.

CHAPTER SEVEN

"AH, WILDERNESS WERE PARADISE ENOW!"

An Egyptian Spell for a Beautiful Day

May the Sky be opened; may the Earth be opened; may the West be
opened; may the East be opened; may the Chapel of Lower Egypt be
opened. May the Eastern Portals be thrown open for Ra [the Sun God]
when he ascends from the horizon.

Spell #130, Egyptian Book of the Dead

One does not need to seek the Garden of Paradise. It is here in Egypt on Kitchener's Island, surrounded by the incredibly blue waters of the Nile, five hundred miles south of Cairo. With its polished walkways of ice-smooth pink granite and oriental trellises with benches of warm-hued wood, overshadowed by giant royal palms, these were the lush gardens blooming in the wilderness as extolled by the poet Omar Khayyam. One truly expected a genie, escaped from the pages of The Arabian Nights, to step out from behind a flowering purple bush and bow low. Looking like enormous white flowers in bud, live herons roosted in the trees. I think it might have been quite possible for a lion to lie down with a lamb in such a beautiful spot as this. Peace settled amid the foliage and even loud-mouthed tourists spoke in the hushed tones usually reserved for cathedrals. I believe that Kitchener's Gardens is the quietest spot in all Egypt.

Here, there, everywhere scarlet poinsettias bloomed on small trees. I didn't know that the poinsettia was a tree. My only acquaintance with poinsettias were the potted variety which appear at Christmastime. But it is now February – in Egypt – and these fiery stars made our holiday variety look sick and pale in comparison.

Egypt is a land of stone; wood is as precious as a jewel, and the two wooden jewels in this glorious setting are the date palms and the syca-mores. There was a beautiful ancient sycamore here in the Gardens; one that had been growing wide and tall a long time before the gardens were developed by England's Lord Herbert Kitchener in the 1890s. This most venerable tree seemed happy to share its home not only with the native date palms, who sociably lean over to be closer to their neighbor, but also with other – more foreign – palm trees. All of them joined together to create a soft, whispering song as the breeze from the Nile wafted through their fringed leaves.

The Garden's air was filled with sweet scents – not strong, but pleas-antly mindful of the place and the presence. Sandalwood, cedar, and the fragrances of a hundred flowering beauties surrounded us. An arched trel-lis was over-ladened with blossoms the color of orange sherbet. Beyond and to the left were huge purple blooms, which blotted out the view of the river and filled our eyes with lushness. I am not a gardener, nor a botanist, but the sheer abundance of the beauty around me brought tears to my eyes.

Down another walkway of polished stone, a riotous red-orange flower begged to be photographed. Was that a flame tree? I wished I knew, but there were few name tags visible, and my guidebook was brief about Kitchener's Gardens. The blossoms reminded me of the magnolias back home in Virginia, but these flowers were fiery red.

Then, suddenly, the path of mirrored pink stone turned abruptly to rough, and dusty rock stairs that descended to our felucca boat on the river – always returning to the Nile which gave life to this most Enchanted Garden.

CHAPTER EIGHT

SAILING UP THE MAP AND DOWN THE NILE

"The passengers went on board and were shown their accommodations. Since the boat was not full, most of the passengers had accommodations on the promenade deck. The entire forward part of this deck was occupied by an observation salon, all glass enclosed, where the passengers could sit and watch the river before them. One deck below were a smoking room and a small drawing room and on the deck below that, the dining saloon."

When I was an eager fourteen-year-old and starting my freshman year at a new high school, the Reverend Mother in charge welcomed me with this advice: "If you don't understand something, ask questions. Always ask questions." So, I did during my first week in History Class. I asked my new history teacher a question that has since haunted me down through the years.

"Why?" I asked Sister Kondolf, "If gravity pulls rivers down to the sea, why does the Nile River flow UP the map?"

Mass hysterical laughter from my fellow classmates. A small sigh from my history teacher who realized that it was going to be one of those years. Two weeks later, my question appeared in print in the school newspaper under the heading "Classroom Yuks." My innocent question appeared once again in the light-hearted comments that my friends wrote in my freshman yearbook. It re-appeared four years later when our Senior Class History was compiled. It reared its familiar head at my class's Twenty-Fifth reunion, as in "Do you remember when . . .?" It tumbled forth from the lips of my husband on the eve of our departure for our Egyptian Adventure. And, finally, on Day Five of our Ten Glorious Days when we stepped aboard the Sun Boat cruiser at Aswan, I was about to experience for myself sailing Down the Nile and Up the map.

This was my first-ever cruise on anything larger than a canoe. It proved to be everything that I had hoped a pleasure cruise would be, and a good deal more. The Sun Boat was small as Nile cruisers go, only twenty-four cabins, but it closely resembled Agatha Christie's description of the Karnak in her mystery Death on the Nile. Burnished brass sidelights and glossy wooden paneling lined the passageways. Frosted glass doors opened into the comfortable Lounge. Fretted brass lanterns hung over the well-supplied bar. Pink brocaded tablecloths with matching starched napkins stood smartly at each place setting in the Dining Room. Cushioned wicker furniture invited relaxing on the Sun Deck. Has Monsieur Hercule Poirot come aboard yet? Is there a rich heiress here on her honeymoon? Who among our fellow passengers looked as if they might be concealing a tiny little gun and are bent on murderous thoughts? Will there be a body on the Lounge floor by 11 PM? Christie's classic murder mystery lingered in my imagination.

The Sun Boat, a small Nile cruiser with twenty-four cabins, an enclosed lounge with a bar, a dining room, sun deck, swimming pool, and a gift shop.

The Boat Manager greeted us with both enthusiasm and another glass of delicious karkadeh. Karkadeh is made from hibiscus petals, looks like cranberry juice, but tastes sweeter. It is supposed to be a very healthy drink, good for one's blood pressure, digestion, liver, complexion and – if rumor is true – a glassful increases sexual prowess. On hearing that piece of interesting information, some of the gentlemen among our Merry Band drank several refills, and a hearty few drank it every morning at breakfast.

The Boat Manager was not the boat's captain. We never saw the captain, but I presumed that he was on board or else the boat managed to sail itself for 120 miles down the Nile [and UP the map]. The Boat Manager was both our host and our concierge. He assured us that our every whim would be his command. Thankfully, he was not like the comical Boat Manager in the movie Death on the Nile. After all, our Boat Manager was responsible for our dinners and extra towels.

Mohammed's eyes sparkled and his moustache twitched when we asked him about the boat's captain. "He is also my cousin," he deadpanned.

We nodded. Of course! This is Egypt where they have large families. Who could tell?

Our cabin aboard the Sun Boat was everything that could be desired when one is cruising down the Nile. There was a never-ending supply of bottled water on the bedside table, lots of coat hangers in the tiny closet, a charming print of the Temple of Isis at Philae on the wall, and a full can of bug spray in our cozy bathroom. Our "porthole" was a large picture window, and the view was always magnificent. In fact, the view from our picture window had probably not changed much since the time when Queen Cleopatra took her Roman boyfriend, Mark Anthony up the Nile on a little three-month jaunt in her purple-tasseled sailboat. That was a cruise in right-royal style. The never-changing scenery glided by our window, mile after mile, as if it were being scrolled across a giant screen.

The lush green of the riverside cultivation gave away suddenly to the dry and barren desert. It was literally possible to stand with one foot in a field of moist green clover while the other foot was embedded in dry sand. The ancient Egyptians called this contrast the Red and Black lands. The black is the rich, dark earth that the Nile brought down from Africa. The desert's reddish, iron-based tints are a little harder to describe. Sometimes the sand and rock looked beige, then burnt sienna, then pink. Other times, the desert seemed white or ivory in color, then suddenly it would turn to pink, then lavender, then violet, and finally to purple when the twilight suddenly descended. Taken altogether, and from the air especially, Egypt's barren wastes do look as if they had a reddish hue.

Nor does the desert look the same in all places. In the south, called Upper Egypt [or down] the map, the desert undulates towards the horizon, in huge, powdery dunes. They are something like the dunes at the tip of Cape Cod in Massachusetts, or Jockey's Ridge on the coastline at Nags Head in North Carolina. Midway between Aswan in the south and Cairo in the north is the city of Luxor. Across the river from Luxor is Thebes, and the Valleys of The Kings and The Queens. There, the desert looks more like the Badlands of the Dakotas in the American west with rocky escarpments and a hard-packed desert floor. The Valleys themselves are like nothing else on earth – more like a moonscape or a Martian desert – and extremely hot in temperature, even in February.

Cities in Egypt are few and far between, but clustered along the riverbanks are little villages with small houses made of mud brick, dried to a chalky-gray color by the sun. The riverside scenes, as we sailed past them, looked like villages that were straight out of the Bible. The ever-present date palms hovered around them, bending maternally over these simple dwellings as if trying to shield the family inside from the blistering sun. At the river's edge, we saw gaggles of small children shrieking with laughter and splashing each other as they went about the business of washing the family's donkey. The donkey stood up to his fetlocks in the cool water and waited with commendable patience for his bath.

Farther down the river, a farmer, his loose galabia hitched above his knees, urged his long-horned bullock to plow an ever-diminishing square of the dark earth. Around the next bend in the river, other farmers loaded up flatboats with long stalks of freshly cut sugar cane. The cane was hauled on the backs of donkeys to the riverside from the fields beyond our vision. These little animals were so loaded down with the cane stalks, it looked like the bundles had sprouted four little legs and walked themselves to the river.

The Sun Boat rounded another river bend and the ruins of a columned temple appeared. Our Merry Band, seated upstairs on the sun deck, had been waiting, cameras in hand, for just this moment. We have arrived at Kom Ombo, the first of the riverside temples on our itinerary. As our boat glided up to the dock, a tiny little girl led her equally tiny baby donkey to the road where we tourists would pass by them on our way to the temple. This adorable child, dressed in bright-colored clothing, and wearing colorful beads and bangles was the youngest entrepreneur whom we had yet encountered. She positioned herself and her little donkey in the middle of the road, and she was ready to pose for our cameras. She kept her shaggy partner interested in the enterprise by feeding him handfuls of clover.

Meanwhile, the Sun Boat's crew tied our boat to the dock with swift efficiency. The gangplank was lowered, but before any of us could alight, a thick Oriental carpet was rolled out down the plank, across the quay and up the steps to the road. Nothing like making a grand entrance for the entertainment of the gathering crowd of townsfolk. I half-expected that we would be hand-carried to the very gates of the temple.

In the meantime, the little girl and her little donkey patiently waited. Of course, our shipmates stopped, and were soon crouching in various uncomfortable positions, while they tried to get the most perfect picture of Little Girl with Donkey. The young lady, no more than six or seven years old, knew her business. She helpfully directed the American tourists for the best photo angles – all for the price of three Egyptian pounds [approximately a dollar in American currency] per person. In another ten years, she will probably be a fashion model – if her father lets her. He stood quietly to one side of the road, and he watched his manipulative offspring with a gentle smile and a touch of fatherly pride. This beautiful child was probably the family's breadwinner. This is Egypt and Western sensibilities have no place here. At least, the little girl's clothes were clean, her hair was brushed to a shine, and both she and the donkey looked well-fed. The child's grasp of English, and probably several other languages as well, was amazing. Also, she had a good head for figures, and she knew exactly how to make the correct change. All things considered. she was probably a lot better off than a lot of American inner-city kids twice her age.

Before we moved on to the temple, Mohammed gathered us around him for a special announcement. "Tomorrow night, the boat's crew will give a party for you."

We expressed murmurs of surprise and delight.

"It will be a galabia party, very traditional," he continued.

There was more murmuring as most of us were confused. There must be some sort of reason for the party.

Mohammed's eyes twinkled. "It is polite for all guests – you, ladies and gentlemen – to wear the native galabia."

Ah ha! The light began to dawn on us.

"Fortunately," Mohammed continued with a wide smile. "I know of a place where you will get the best price for a galabia. Very good bargains." Then Mohammed sprang his punchline. "For you only, the best price. The salesman is my cousin. This way, please."

All Nile cruise boats host Galabia Parties. No tourist sailing on the Nile can escape one, unless they want to forgo an excellent dinner, and hide in their cabins for the entire evening. Most of our group were too polite to do that. Besides, we had come to Egypt to experience something different. A Galabia Party is definitely "something different"; it is completely out of one's comfort zone, yet a good deal safer than a visit to the local hubbly-bubbly cafe.

Galabias are the long, loose gowns that many Egyptian men usually wear. Egyptian women, at least the few whom we saw, wore versions of the men's galabias, but that was a moot point when it came to tourists being cajoled into buying one for a Galabia Party. Galabias come in all colors, designs, and sleeve lengths, and they seemed tailored to drag at least six inches on the floor. I tried to explain to Mohammed's very excited cousin that I was only five-foot-two and had short legs. No problem, I was assured. I was getting a very good deal. My galabia still dragged on the floor – but I had paid the "best price." I should have wised up and gotten a child's size.

Marty absolutely loved his galabia. His fit him.

I am convinced that our crew always throw a Galabia Party for every boatload of gullible tourists, because we are their entertainment for the week. That evening, decked out in Mohammed's cousin's inventory, we arrived in the Lounge for the pre-dinner cocktail party. Together with a second tour group, who were also enjoying their own Ten Glorious Days spoken in German while sailing onboard the Sun Boat, our Merry Band looked like a crowd of over-grown children, dressed in our nightgowns, and waiting for our evening milk and graham crackers. It is no wonder that the crew smiled so broadly at us. We must have looked very comical. American and German dignity was covered up under large, flowing gowns from head to toe aboard the Good Ship Sun Boat that night. Nevertheless, all of us proved to be Good Sports. Many of the women in our company had added veils and bangles to their ensembles. The one child on our boat, a winsome German lass of about ten, even dressed her teddy bear in a mini galabia. She deserved an extra helping of honey baklava dessert for that.

Despite our best attempts to look as exotic as possible, it was Mohammed who outshone us all. Obviously, he did not patronize his cousin's galabia shop. Normally, Mohammed wore black trousers, a white shirt and often a black cape. This night, Mohammed appeared dressed like the Sheik of Arabia. With his twinkling brown eyes and a flashing smile under his thick, black moustache, his attire looked perfect. The sisters, Polly and Ginger effervesced with flattering compliments, and Mohammed lapped it up like cream. He absolutely made everyone's evening perfect – especially for George and our other hard-core shutterbugs.

Entertainment during our delicious dinner was Nubian drumming and singing – mostly drumming. Our crewmen, like most of the crews on the Nile tour boats, were Nubians from the southern border of Egypt. There was more of the African influence in their physical looks, in their music, and in their crafts, which were sold primarily in Aswan. The drumming sounded like it was straight out of the jungle, while their singing was rather monotonous, and was composed of very long lyrics in Arabic. I found myself chewing my dinner in time with the rhythm of the music.

After dinner, the first entertainment was a series of silly games that the men of both tour groups were enticed into playing. Marty took part in a potato race that involved having a large potato, attached to a long string, and tied around his waist. Then, racing two other guys from both tour groups, he had to knock down as many wooden dolls that lined the floor as possible by using his hips to swing the potato between his legs. The race was hilarious to watch. I was especially proud that Marty beat out both Fred from our group and one of the gentlemen from the German tour by knocking over the most wooden dolls. Marty's prize was one of the dolls as a memento. The highlight of the evening was the re-enactment of a Nubian wedding party, which, we were told, could go on and on for days. Sandi, dressed in a beautiful white and gold galabia, had been talked into portraying the bride, and she ended up dancing in the center of the lounge by herself. For something so impromptu, Sandi did an excellent job. Her husband, Vin, especially enjoyed the show.

Thankfully, our celebration only lasted several hours instead of days. After Sandi's solo, there was a lot more drumming, more singing, and most of the audience were cajoled into dancing. I love to dance. I even enjoyed Nubian dancing once I got the hang of it. Basically, it was a step-kick, step-kick in a circle, and one danced this movement, without stopping for water or breathing, for the next twenty minutes. It was like low-impact aerobics. Endurance was the key. What made the whole evening worthwhile was our Nubian crew. These young men could really gyrate. In fact, they were some of the best dancers whom I have ever had the pleasure of partnering.

At the end of the evening's festivities, a group photo was taken by a local photographer who had been hired for the occasion. The remainders of our Merry Band, those who had not sneaked away to their staterooms, as well as Mohammed, the Boat Manager, and the Crew all crowded together in one big, happy, sweaty mass to be immortalized on film for posterity – at only five Egyptian pounds per photo. By midnight, the Crew still looked as fresh as daisies and were extremely pleased with themselves. Mohammed looked regal. The Boat Manager looked relieved and we surviving tourists looked exhausted, bedraggled and slightly shell-shocked from all the drumming. On the other hand, that group photo, which was displayed the following morning in the Lounge after breakfast, was a point of pride for certain members of our Merry Band, for it proved who were the real die-hards of our group.

Later that memorable evening, after we shed our sweaty galabias, taken showers and turned out our light, Marty whispered to me, "Look out the window."

Ever since we had boarded the Sun Boat, we were always saying to each other, "Look out the window." This time he put his finger to his lips and indicated that I should look out and down. Could it be a rare crocodile surfacing?

No. A huge, fat moon had risen, turning the river into a pathway of shimmering silver. The Sun Boat had been tied up for the night at a small sand bar. Between our ship and the shore, a small river skiff had tied up, and had attached its lines to ours. In the center of the little boat, two men sat cross-legged, facing each other, and socially shared puffs from a large hubbly-bubbly water pipe that was positioned between them. The elder man, wearing a turban and sporting a flowing white beard, smoked in silence, nodding his head in agreement to his companion who made occasional quiet comments, punctuated by long pauses. The light from our Lounge on the deck below us spilled onto the smokers, creating a Rembrandt effect. Marty and I watched them for a few more moments, then we withdrew, feeling as if we had been eavesdropping on an extremely personal conversation.

"I wish I could have taken a picture of that," I sighed as I crawled under the sheets.

"You did," replied my husband, who was already half-asleep. "You will have it locked forever in your memory."

Early the next morning, we did get the picture of a lifetime that was "worth a thousand words." A thumping, bumping sound and the jiggling of the bedsprings woke me from the best sleep that I had yet enjoyed in Egypt. Generally, I do not sleep well in strange beds, but all the dancing and drumming of the previous evening had knocked me out. Our cabin was still dark, and the glowing face of my travel clock said it was 5:25 am. I do not accept the truth that there is life before seven o'clock in the morning.

Unfortunately, I married a bright and chirpy Early Bird, who was now in the process of trying to put on his pants while taking pictures out of the window without waking me. He failed miserably.

"Are we on fire?" I asked, opening both eyes. There was an alarming orange glow seeping between the drawn curtains.

"Look out the window!" he hissed, pulling on his shoes without socks.

"It's 5:30 in the morning!" I moaned, burying my head in the stack of pillows.

Marty merely pulled both covers and all the pillows off my protesting body, then he dragged me out of the bed.

"Look out the window," he repeated, as he looped the camera strap around his neck. "You'll never see anything like this again!"

So, I opened both eyes again, and looked out as "the sun comes up like thunder," according to Rudyard Kipling.

The French writer, Flaubert described an Egyptian sunrise best. "The palms are black as ink, the sky is red; the Nile has the look of a lake of molten steel," he wrote, when he saw this same incredible, glorious, mystical, magical dawn in March 1850. Mere words, not even Flaubert's, can truly convey the beauty that unfolded before us that cool, early morning.

Up to this moment, I had been disappointed by Egyptian sunsets. Purple twilights happened suddenly here, instead of the long, lingering golden sunsets of tropical islands, so I had not given much thought to sunrises, expecting them to be somewhat similar. I was completely wrong. This sunrise took away my breath. For once, I was totally speechless, just drinking in the slow, stately arrival of Amon-Ra, the Egyptian sun god.

Marty, with his camera firmly in hand, rushed out of our cabin, heading for the Sun Deck. Where else could one properly greet the sun? I chose to admire the beauty of the moment from the comfort of my own bed, but Marty was right. I have never seen the like of that dawn again.

On our last evening aboard the Sun Boat, the crew outdid themselves. I did not expect a Formal Dinner. The tour brochure never said a word about dressing for a formal dinner. I thought that the idea of "dressing for dinner" had gone down with the Titanic, but on the menu board posted outside the Dining Room were the words "Formal Dinner Tonight." And that didn't mean our galabias. I had packed the last word in safari gear: khaki pants, loose blouses, bandanas, stout shoes, bedroom slippers and a pair of sneakers — even my bona fide pith helmet and a roll of campers' toilet paper. Thanks to Mohammed's cousin, I now possessed the second-to-the-last-word in galabias. Formal Attire was nowhere to be found on my packing list or in my suitcase.

Marty was no help at all in this situation. He had packed a tie and a clean white shirt, neatly folded in the bottom of his bag. He couldn't understand my problem. I did the only thing I could think of doing in this emergency – accessorize. I draped my one and only dressy blouse with every bead and bangle that seven days of serious gift shopping had accumulated. Necklaces, earrings, bracelets, and rings on almost every finger. Then I polished up my knee boots, tied a bright-colored scarf around the waist of my divided skirt, added another scarf around my neck and shoulders, and, looking like Amanda Peabody, heroine of Elizabeth Peter's Egyptian mystery series, I declared myself ready for dinner.

What a dinner it was! The candle-lit tables gleamed with polished silver. The starched brocade linens crackled. Our waiters, who, only two nights ago had entertained us wearing turbans and galabias, were now resplendent in brass buttoned red jackets and black bow ties. At the end of the soup course, all the candles in the room were extinguished, leaving us literally and figuratively in the dark. Then, over the stereo speakers came the stirring strains of the "Triumphal March" from the opera Aida. The kitchen doors flew open, and the first waiter entered holding two enormous flaming torches, which he paraded around the Dining Room with a great deal of flair and fire. Following close behind him were four other waiters, each one bearing several plates – our main course: Steak Parisian decorated with lemon halves and green leaves. Each half lemon held a lighted candle in the center. Soon the Dining Room took on a warm, magical glow. It was an incredible, breath-taking, and dramatic presentation. The food, of course, was delicious.

But it was the dessert that won our loudest applause and flashing cameras. Our table candles were lit again, our dinner plates were whisked away and then, from the kitchen, came a familiar sound.

"Oh, dear Lord," Marty murmured under his breath. "Not more drumming!"

The Sun Boat's farewell dessert – yellow pyramid cake and a chocolate Sphinx.

Indeed, it was more drumming, as the musician burst out from the kitchen. He was followed by the chef, whom we had never seen. This Master of the Galley paraded around the room, proudly carrying a large tray bearing his ultimate creation – three yellow iced cakes in the shapes of the pyramids of Giza guarded by a chocolate Sphinx, his lines defined with white icing. After all the guests had applauded and taken pictures, this mouth-watering confection was carved by the Boat Manager. I was slightly disappointed that the Boat Manager didn't use a bejeweled scimitar instead of a mere cake knife. And so, stuffed with cake and the sugared Chocolate Sphinx, our cruise on the Nile came to its never-to-be-forgotten end.

The next morning, we disembarked at the town of Luxor, and prepared to take the bus that would whisk us to the airport where EgyptAir would fly us, in due time, back to Cairo, Allah be willing. As I waited for Marty to finish his farewells to the Boat Manager and to give him the customary tip for his excellent services these past five days, I noticed a small dry leaf lying at my feet. I picked it up and tossed it into the Nile. The great river swept up my little bark which would float down past two hundred miles of desert, through the heart of Cairo, then it would thread its way through the muddy fingers of the Delta until it finally emptied into the Mediterranean Sea.

You were right, Sister Kondolf, but then, I always knew you were. Now, I had seen it for myself: the Nile truly does flow up the map and down to the sea.

CHAPTER NINE

FOR YOU, THE BEST PRICE!

"**H**ey, American Lady! Welcome to Alaska!"

This unusual and attention-grabbing greeting surfaced amid the pushing, pulsating jumble that is typical of an Egyptian bazaar. It did exactly what this vender in the center of Luxor hoped it would do – stopped us in our dusty tracks. The crafty merchant advanced a little closer and repeated his greeting. "Welcome to Alaska!"

This is but one example of the famous Egyptian sense of humor. He knew that Alaska's climate was the opposite of his own, but, on the other hand, he now had gotten our attention.

He pointed to his over-loaded stall with the swelling pride of owner-ship. "You look here . . . just look! No charge . . . no problem!"

He gestured to us madly to keep our attention from wandering, because the neighboring venders now saw that he had gotten a bite. To them, we are "rich Americans." All Americans visiting Egypt must be rich, the merchants reasoned, because it cost a lot of money for Americans to travel all the way across the Atlantic Ocean to the African continent. Each merchant also reasoned that, in the divine order of things, we, being so rich, could afford to share our wealth, and what better place to start this money sharing, then at his stall? The only unconcerned creature in this teeming marketplace was a tan-colored dog with mangy fur, who slept disdainfully in the exact center of the market's thoroughfare. His ear twitched away the hovering flies.

The merchant hopped about his stall. "You look, you buy. I give you very nice price."

His "r's" rolled musically off his tongue. His smile was a yard wide. His wares, baking in the desert sun, were just like everyone else's wares: blue beads ["Real turquoise, you see? No plastic!"], black Bastet cats, the Falcon God in assorted sizes, brilliant-hued packages of brocaded table-cloths and napkins, mother-of-pearl inlaid boxes, greenish scarabs, and brass trays. No price tags.

With a grin, Marty began his bargaining in earnest. In Egypt, bar-gaining is the vendor's pleasure – and the tourist's pain. The salesman had waited all morning for this moment, he led us to believe. Bargaining is the Egyptians' favorite pastime, and they are masters of the art.

"Best price, I give you best price – because I am honest."

This vendor was a whirlwind of activity, spreading sweet-smell-ing sandalwood oil on the back of my hand, fastening strings of beads around my neck, and holding up a smudged mirror for me to see the effect. Meanwhile, he talked a mile a minute to Marty, the man of the family. What the vendor didn't know was that Marty had spent a year working for the U.S. Navy in Saudi Arabia, and he had learned the art of Middle Eastern bargaining.

"Forty pounds," the vendor suggested, his arm swept around the small mound of goods that he had laid out at our feet.

"Fifteen pounds," my husband countered. I tried not to look anxious, even though I really wanted all of it as gifts for everyone on our Christmas list. A small but growing crowd of men sucked in their collective breaths with appreciation and respect. This American knew how to play the game. The vendor acted as if he were suffering heartburn. He turned to me.

"Handmade, lady. See? All handmade." He tried to drape a dusty galabia over me, then he pressed a darling statuette of a black cat into my hand. Marty kept a straight face. I struggled not to say anything. Women were not supposed to speak to a vendor if her husband was present. This was the way the game was played.

"Twenty pounds." Marty looked bored, as if he were losing interest. The watching crowd grew.

I bit my tongue. I really, really wanted the cat. In fact, I wanted several cats for gifts. The nearby merchants licked their lips and rubbed their fingers, calculating how to open negotiations, just in case we walked away from the first salesman, who was now all but throwing himself and several dusty prayer rugs at our feet.

"Twenty-five pounds – everything – twenty-five pounds." The vendor sweated profusely, and he reminded us that he was the sole provider for his parents, his many cousins, and the many, many children in his family.

The crowd grew silent as Marty shook his head. "Twenty-two pounds," he offered. He was playing the game well. The crowd looked at my husband with more respect.

The merchant made a strangled sound in the back of his throat as if he were dying. "Twenty-three pounds?"

Everyone surrounding us breathed as one as they waited to see what Marty would do.

Slowly, Marty nodded. "Twenty-three pounds for the beads and three cats."

Huge smile on the face of the vendor. Huge smiles on the faces in the crowd. The American had made a good price. The vendor shook hands with Marty to seal the deal. He shook hands with me to seal the deal. I wondered if he would shake hands with everyone in the crowd to seal the deal. Pound notes were exchanged. They were filthy and had seen much better days. I tucked our purchases into my canvas shopping bag, and we moved on.

The closest merchant pursued us. "Eh, American lady! For you! Best price!"

Before we flew off to Egypt, our nearest and dearest had given us wish lists for things that they hoped we would buy for them. A prayer rug for our son. A hubbly-bubbly water pipe for our new son-in-law. "Just something gold" for our daughter. More "somethings" for the secretaries at Marty's office. Gifts for our three nieces and seven godchildren. Postcards to send to forty-nine people whose addresses I had typed onto self-stick labels. A good-luck scarab for my hairdresser. Egyptian cigarettes for the smokers on our list. Fragile glass perfume bottles for my girlfriends. And finally, a painting on a piece of real papyrus for me. In short, we were primed for some serious shopping up and down the Nile. Our most interesting adventure in shopping happened in Luxor, which is a charming city midway between Cairo and Nubia. All we wanted to buy was a prayer rug. It was a simple enough item on our list. Egyptians prayed five times a day while facing Mecca. Prayer rugs were plentiful.

The first order of business was locating a rug shop. The doorman outside the Isis Hotel waved us down the street towards a shop he said he knew. After thanking him with some baksheesh [tip], we were off. I could feel a surge of excitement running through Marty's veins as we fled across the main throughfare, avoiding honking tour buses, overloaded donkey carts, fresh donkey poop, potholes, more sleeping dogs and ancient automobiles on suicide missions. This was our Eighth Glorious Day in Egypt and Marty's grasp of Arabic had returned. Normally, he hated shopping, and he avoided American malls like the plague. But shopping that included bargaining was a whole different thing. It was the lure and the challenge of the game that enticed him into Luxor's shopping district.

Of all the bazaars, stalls, and shops that we stumbled into and out of during our Ten Glorious Days, the most beautiful and fantastic one was the Isis Perfume Market located in Luxor. This small emporium, about the size of a large American bathroom, seemed to be made entirely of glass and mirrors which reflected the hundreds of tiny gleaming perfume bottles in a myriad of dazzling jewel colors: ruby reds, sapphire blues, emerald greens, diamond whites, amber yellows, and amethyst purples. Each delicate vial, some standing no taller than three inches, had been handblown into a hundred different shapes. It was a fantasy city in miniature, all highlighted in gold leaf. It was the poetry of the Rubaiyat of Omar Khayyam spun into glass. I was enchanted; my husband, on the other hand, was a nervous wreck. In fact, he was afraid to move inside the tiny shop.

"Don't sneeze," Marty cautioned me as he backed out onto the street. Mumbling "I have to cash some more travelers' checks, I'll meet you out here," he fled with a sigh of relief, leaving me to buy twenty bottles.

I got down to some of my own serious bargaining with the saleslady, who was as petit and as jewel-like as her wares. She spoke very good, schoolgirl English, and she smiled a lot. A half hour later, I was the proud owner of not twenty, but thirty perfume bottles in assorted sizes and colors – a real treasure trove. Marty's eyes grew quite large when I met him across the dusty street.

"Thirty bottles?" he sputtered. "What are you going to do with thirty little empty bottles that will probably shatter before we can get them back to Cairo? Are you planning to open your own souk?"

I remained calm. Marty often resorted to the question of packing when it came to my shopping trips. It was his one line of defense against my flights of fancy and excesses. However, in this case, I had an answer. Two-thirds of my purchases were for several of our shipmates on the Sun Boat, who had asked me to "pick up some bottles" for them when they had heard where we were going. By now, Marty's bargaining powers of dealing with the friendly natives was near legend among the Merry Band. I told him that getting our own nine bottles back home in one piece would be no problem. What was the point of having laundry if you couldn't use it to wrap up your breakables?

Our next stop was the rug shop that practically yawned at our feet. The entrance was below the street level and inside; we could see wall-to-wall rugs of every hue and size. With a huge smile on his face, Marty plunged down the stairs and through the open door. I followed him inside what seemed like the Black Hole of Calcutta. I couldn't help but wonder if this particular shop was really a good idea. Several men, seated on cushions around a water pipe, looked up from their smoking and smiled at me. Then they smiled to each other.

Ignoring them, Marty and I began to paw through a stack of small prayer rugs near the shop's entrance. No price tags were visible.

"You do not want those rugs, sir," said a smooth voice behind us. The shopkeeper who looked like Ali Baba with fearsome moustaches and a flashing, wide smile full of brilliant white teeth, waved away the stack of rugs. "Machine made . . . not good enough for you, sir! You come this way. I show you good rugs."

"This way" proved to be an enclosed back room. The walls fairly dripped with carpets. The floor was piled six or seven deep with rugs. I wondered if we should have removed our shoes. The salesman escorted us to a low divan at the far end of the room. It was pouffed and pillowed in many brilliant-hued patterns that I can only describe as "Moorish." It was very comfortable to sit on — Arabian Nights at high noon on Luxor's main drag.

"Mint tea?" Ali Baba murmured, looking at me. "So refreshing on such a hot day. Would the lady wish for some mint tea?"

No, the lady did not wish for some mint tea. At this point, the lady's inner antennae were twanging a warning, and she was wishing she could get out of there. The hairs on the back of my neck started to quiver.

However, Marty was hell-bent on getting a few prayer rugs. Mr. Baba also had an agenda which he soon demonstrated by sitting down next to me on the divan – sitting very, very close to me on the divan.

I have natural dark blond hair. I had always heard that blonds were supposed to have more fun, and I think that may have been what this owner of the Forty Thieves Rug Emporium had in his predatory mind. I had to give the guy some credit, he was one smooth operator. He managed to keep Marty busy looking at rug after rug, while, at the same time, he and I played "Musical Chairs" down the length of the long divan. Didn't Marty even notice that I was being stalked for the white slave trade? Did he pay any attention to my squeaks about how late we were going to be for lunch back on the boat? No, he was busy making a "good price" for a flying carpet.

And I certainly didn't like the way Mr. Ali Baba purred, "For you, Lady, best price."

"The best price for me, all right," I thought to myself as Ali Baba's arm crept around behind me. His strong cologne was enchanting – just what you'd expect an abductor would wear. I half expected that at any moment, when Marty's back was turned, I would be knocked unconscious, bound, gagged, and bundled into a large wicker basket that had recently been vacated by some cobra in the entertainment business. I would awake, dull and groggy, to find myself strapped to a camel's back and on my way to the harem of a lonely sheik in a remote desert fortress, far, far to the south. There, I would be forced to wear golden bracelets and a gauzy pajama with a bare midriff as I faced a Fate Worse Than Death.

Yes, I was a little bit over-wrought, as well as being a little over the age of forty. I'm not only blond, but also green-eyed, fair-skinned, in good health and I have all my teeth. Lonely sheiks in remote desert fortresses aren't too picky, I imagined. Meanwhile, my sweet husband would never notice if I just disappeared. He was still deciding rug patterns.

Ali Baba finally made his move. His hand covered my knee.

I gulped, jumped up from the divan and crossed over to Marty. "Great rug," I muttered to my clueless spouse. "Let's get it and get out of here! Hele mai," I added, using the Hawaiian words we had learned when the Navy had stationed us at Pearl Harbor during the early days of our marriage. "Hele mai" meant "let's go" to us, and we often used those code words at long cocktail parties when one of us wanted to go home.

Meanwhile, Ali Baba, the would-be abductor, sighed, and turned his full attention to Marty. The bargaining began in earnest. I stayed well out of reach. At the end of what seemed like a lifetime, the "best price" had been reached. The bargain was sealed, and handshakes exchanged. Ali then advanced towards me.

"A kiss," he murmured, "For good luck."

The next thing I knew, I was being bussed by those huge moustaches, first on one cheek, then on the other. Meanwhile, my husband and my protector just stood there grinning and holding out his VISA card. It was on the tip of my tongue to inform both gentlemen that I was NOT part of the deal. I stalked out of that Den of Iniquity, avoiding the interested gaze of the hubbly-bubbly smokers, and I occupied myself with studying the pile of rugs nearest the front door.

"That guy!" I steamed as we trotted back to the Sun Boat with the prayer rug under Marty's arm and thirty glass perfume bottles in my tote bag. "He . . . he . . . "

"Interesting experience," Marty calmly remarked.

"Interesting!" I yelped, side-stepping a kid on a motorbike. "I was expecting to be kidnapped at any moment, drugged with mint tea and rolled up in a carpet."

"What a shame!" Marty said with a huge grin. "I'm so sorry you were disappointed."

Incidentally, our son loved his prayer rug.

CHAPTER TEN

THE OTHER HOLY LAND

t's not stretching the truth to say that visiting Egypt is a religious experience. It truly is a Holy Land – not the Holy Land of Israel, but a Holy Land, none-the-less. Religion is the heart of Egypt. The desert sands are steeped in it.

Consider the ancient monuments that we had traveled over nine thousand miles to see. These are the monuments that I had dreamed about most of my life. What were they? Temples, places of worship, rock tombs covered with striking paintings and hieroglyphics depicting gods and goddesses, as well as the story of Creation, the Resurrection of Osiris, the Last Judgement of the Heart. For thousands of years, the Egyptians toiled on behalf of their gods, and the ancient people preserved their religious beliefs for posterity on the walls of their tombs.

Enter Alexander the Great, who was Greek, and who superimposed his pantheon of gods upon the Egyptians. The Greco-Egyptian temples of Kom Ombo, Philae and Esna are some of the most beautiful examples of the hybrid order. Later, Julius Caesar came, saw, and was conquered by Cleopatra, a descendant of Alexander. Roman gods were added to the holy crowd.

During the following centuries, many religions were practiced side-by-side. In the early Roman period, a small Jewish community established itself in Alexandria. Later, the Christian Coptics fled to the outskirts of the Egyptian deserts, where they could practice their schismatic form of Christianity in peace. Islam took the country by storm in the late 600's. Mosques grew up cheek-to-jowl next to the ancient temples. In some places, the mosques were built directly on top of these earlier foundations. Today, Egypt is dotted with mosques, great and small, and the Islamic religion is devoutly observed. The daily calls to prayer can be heard in every corner of Egypt, thanks to the modern invention of electronic loudspeakers. The people stop everywhere to kneel and pray, such as that postcard seller in the middle of the Cairo airport. The modern-day Egyptians pray unabashed. They quietly observe the codes and precepts of their faith, and they charitably overlook the tourists' often-insulting ways, such as women wearing short pants and sleeveless tops.

Yes, it is hot in Egypt almost year-round. To us Westerners, it is not a sin for men and women to display their bare knees in public. For the most part, our Moslem hosts were too polite to point out that, in their viewpoint, the Western visitors were practically naked in public. It is no wonder that the Egyptians think that all American women have loose morals; we wear low necklines.

"Here, the Bible is a picture of life today," Flaubert's observation of Egypt in 1850. The people in the countryside still live in the same mud-brick dwellings that their ancestors had lived in for thousands of years. The Hebrews of the Bible must have lived in the same type of mud-brick dwellings when they were enslaved in Egypt during the time of Moses.

Remember Moses? To save him from Pharaoh's cruel edict against first-born Jewish boys, his mother wove a basket made of bullrushes, and she floated her little son down the Nile. Pharaoh's daughter happened to find the basket with the baby caught in another clump of bullrushes—and she raised him as her son. I never knew what bullrushes looked like and figured that they must be something like cattails, which grow near our home in Virginia. It was, therefore, a tremendous surprise, and a scholarly pleasure to finally see real bullrushes. They are tall thick reeds; some grow close to six feet in height. They are found in profusion along the banks and around the islets of the Nile just as they did three thousand years ago. The stalks can be as thick as a grown man's finger and were the color of wheat in February, when we saw them. Blue herons make their waterside nests out of bullrushes. It's no leap of the imagination to see where Moses's mother got her idea of a safe hiding place for her baby.

Then, there was that gripping moment when Moses, now grown to manhood, stood before the Pharaoh, and shouted, "Let my people go!" He wasn't talking to any old, garden-variety pharaoh. Tradition suggests that Moses was yelling at Rameses the Second – otherwise known as Rameses the Great. This pharaoh had a monumental ego, literally; he had erected colossal statues of himself up and down the length of the Nile River. These were the same statues that we had been gaping at for the past five days of our Ten Glorious Days in Egypt. Rameses' statues were the ones that inspired the poet Shelley to write of "the frown, and wrinkled lip and sneer of cold command." And young Moses, fresh out of the wastelands of the desert, had the nerve to say to Rameses the Great, the Colossal, "Let my people go!"

I thought of that defining moment in history when I stood at the base of one of Rameses' thirty-foot statues in the temple of Abu Simbel. These statues are particularly awesome; their half-shut eyes stare down at mere mortals with cold aloofness.

"Looking at these statues [at Abu Simbel] makes one feel so small and rather like an insect," remarked Cornelia Robson, an endearing character in Agatha Christie's murder mystery, Death on the Nile. Staring up into those pitiless eyes, I wondered if I would have had the courage to challenge this man – this awesome ruler. Could I have cried out to him, "Let my people go"?

Moses had a hell of a lot of nerve!

American humorist and author, Mark Twain, who visited Egypt in 1867 and chronicled his adventures throughout the Mediterranean in his book Innocents Abroad, adored the donkeys seen everywhere in Egypt. "Donkeys," Twain praised, "are the omnibuses of Egypt . . . I believe I would rather ride a donkey than any beast in the world. He goes briskly, he puts on no airs, he is docile, although opinionated. Satan himself could not scare him."

There are a lot of paintings of donkeys, some of them famous, that are titled "The Flight into Egypt" featuring the Holy Family, all four of them: Mary, Joseph, the Holy Infant – and the nameless, unsung family donkey. Just like the Egyptian donkeys of today, that patient, lowly creature of the Biblical story was a valued member of the Holy Family. St. Matthew wrote in his Gospel, ". . . he [Joseph] arose and he took the young child and his mother by night and departed into Egypt." Presuming that the Family were fleeing from Bethlehem to the border of modern-day Egypt, it is a journey of roughly forty miles. It would have taken the Holy Family twelve to fourteen hours to walk to Egypt. Once over the border, they would have to travel another hundred or so miles across the desert to reach the Nile. That is a long, hard ride on a donkey's back, and a long walk for the donkey and Joseph. Coptic tradition believes that the Holy Family settled down in the vicinity of Old Cairo. The Abu Serja Church, built around the fourth century, claims to be the oldest Christian church in Egypt. It supposedly marks the place where Jesus, Mary, and Joseph – and the exhausted donkey took shelter.

On the other hand, Joseph could have booked passage for the family on a fast boat to Alexandria, using some of the gold that the Wise Men had given to them. So much for the story of Joseph's donkey crossing the desert, although I am still partial to that idea.

It is interesting to contemplate that Jesus spent many of His earliest, formative years in Egypt. How long did the Holy Family stay in Egypt? How old was Jesus when they returned to Judea? Did Jesus ever wear an

Egyptian boy's kilt? Did Mary ever protect her eyes from the harshness of the sun by lining black kohl around her lids? Were some of the Holy Child's first words spoken in Egyptian? Did Joseph work as a carpenter in a land that had more hard wood two thousand years ago than now? Did he ever make some of the Ptolemaic mummy cases of that period? Did Joseph fashion some of the lovely chairs with clawed feet and winged arms? Was Jesus old enough to learn senet, a popular chess-like game? Did He ever write His name inside a cartouche? The Bible gives no answers to these questions, but it does indicate that Jesus was well-educated by the time when He was twelve years old. He had stayed behind in Jerusalem, where His anxious parents found Him in the Temple, surrounded by the learned scholars. Jesus could write. The Gospels tell how He wrote in the dust the sins of the men who wanted to stone the woman taken in adultery. Where did Jesus' education start? In Alexandria, the seat of ancient thought and once the home of the most comprehensive library in the ancient world? What influence did Egypt have on the Founder of Christianity?

Since our return from Egypt, the figures of our Christmas Nativity set have taken on a whole new meaning for me. Our little set is strictly vintage Woolworth's Five and Dime, made in Italy out of papier-mache. I now realize that the ox should have longer horns, like the ones we saw pulling a plow in a riverside cane field. Most of the Nativity sets have camels that are two-humped, but the Arabian camel is single humped. Tradition tells us that at least two of the Wise Men were from the African continent. Melchior is thought to be Arab, while Balthasar is said to be Ethiopian. Surely, they would have been astride one-humped beasts. Caspar, the third Wise Man, is said to have journeyed from the Indian sub-continent, so one could give him the two-humped variety of camel.

There are always a lot of sheep in the Christmas story, but I have never heard of a goat visiting the manger in Bethlehem. Goats abound in Egypt, producing feta cheese. Everyone in Egypt enjoys eating feta cheese. Surely, there were goats among the sheep on that first Christmas night.

Our stable looks like something found in fourteenth century France, complete with a thatched roof. Where is the plain, square mud-brick hut with a large opening on one side? Where is the bright green clover for the animals to eat? Hay is European fodder in the wintertime. Why doesn't Joseph hold a clay oil lamp, instead of a waxen candle lantern?

If the shepherds and angels played music for the Holy Child on that first Christmas night, they didn't use Renaissance instruments. There should be flutes, finger cymbals, tambourines, and a lot of drumming. The Little Drummer Boy should shed his Bavarian costume and get a larger, flatter drum. And I would get rid of the pastel-colored robes that all the figures wear. Put the men and boys in colorful, striped galabias, and dress the angels in modest versions of harem dancers. Let's be honest, the angels had to catch the attention of those sleepy shepherd boys in the middle of the night. Also, it would be nice to find some tiny bells and red tassels for the camels. Finally, there should be some tiny bags holding a little gold chain, some small bits of frankincense and myrrh for the camels to carry.

Our modern, commercial Nativity sets owe a great deal to the paintings of Donatello and Raphael rather than to historical accuracy.

Egypt is truly a Holy Land. Joseph, the one who owned the Coat of Many Colors in the Old Testament, was first a slave, then later, the Prime Minister of Pharaoh. Potiphar, who initially purchased young Joseph, no doubt got the "best price" for such a young, healthy, intelligent and, as Potiphar's wife later discovered, handsome slave. Joseph's enormous family, the twelve tribes of Israel, moved to Egypt and lived there for over four hundred years, baking both bread and bricks along the banks of the Nile. Joseph's descendant, Moses grew to become a great lord in Egypt before he parted the Red Sea and took his people back to their homeland in Judea. As the French traveler Flaubert observed in 1850, "Here, the Bible is a picture of life today."

CHAPTER ELEVEN

TEMPLES, TOMBS, AND PAINTED ROOMS

G oing north down the Nile [and up the map] was Philae, another temple like Abu Simbel, which had been removed above the encroaching waters of the Aswan Dam. Reconstructed on a higher, neighboring island, this beautiful little temple was dedicated to Isis, the Egyptian goddess of Love. This same temple is also sacred to Hathor, the goddess whose special province was the hearth and home of the people. The feminists in our group especially liked this deity. Mohammed explained why the Egyptian women were so often depicted on the walls and tombs as seated behind the man, with her arms outstretched around him.

"No, she is not looking for his wallet," he joked with us. "She is protecting her lord and master. With her embrace, she will create for him a safe home. She is, in fact, his house."

"House" is the word that means "wife" in ancient Egyptian, Mohammed assured us. We moved on, taking photographs of this enchanting "house." The goddess Hathor is occasionally pictured on the walls as a beautiful woman with very large eyes, and a set of cow ears protruding out from under an elaborate wig. This is good, Mohammed instructed us as George's videocam whirred. We ladies were assured that if you are told you have cow eyes, it is very complimentary. Unfortunately, mine are green and tend to squint in the sun.

Pause to use the Ladies' Room at the Temple of Philae.

I used the Ladies' Rooms every chance I got on this trip because you never know when you are going to need one when you are a hundred miles from nowhere. I could write the Good Loo Guide of Egypt. Most of them have plumbing that works. Most of them are clean – by Middle Eastern standards and, in February, they do not smell very much. All of Egypt's Ladies' Rooms have attendants who dispenses two small squares of crinkly toilet paper for a "tip" of an Egyptian pound [roughly 33 cents]. This was why I carried my own supply of softer, cleaner camper's toilet paper, although I still had to pay a pound, so that the Attendant would not lose face or lose her/his temper. Oh, yes, Egyptian Restroom attendants are an Equal Opportunity Occupation. It is interesting to note here, that the women attendants were some of the very few women whom we saw in Egypt outside of Cairo. Women are supposed to stay at home with the children and donkeys.

There is almost always a line waiting to use the facilities. I got into some of the most interesting conversations while waiting my turn in the Ladies' lines, except at the Museum of Antiquities in Cairo where everyone talked at once, but no one spoke the same language. Ever notice that the guys never have a line in the Gents loo? At Philae, I quietly bemoaned to one of our Merry Band about the lack of tissues, and especially, paper towels – which are universally nonexistent. Then the lady standing behind me spoke up in English.

"That's because paper is very dear here. Egypt is a land with no trees," she gently explained as we shuffled forward toward the stalls. She told us that she had been living with her family in Cairo for the past year, and she had obviously made a small study into the subject of Bathroom Tissue. "If any paper were to be left unattended in the loos, it would disappear in a moment!"

Food for thought as we inched our way across the uneven tile floor. Egypt had invented paper centuries ago. Papyrus was used for all important documents. Papyrus – that is where we get the name "paper." And now, in this modern land where real papyrus plants are few and wood is almost non-existent, all paper products are imported, which is why paper is costly.

"It's about time!" one of the husbands in our group bellowed as we ladies returned from our journey into Restroom No-Man's Land. My husband, who is used to these long waits, merely cocked his head, and smiled sweetly at me.

"Come along, my Little House with the Cow Eyes," he murmured.

Our next stop on our tour was the unfinished obelisk at Aswan. One doesn't view it from afar. One stands on it, because some distant pharaoh in the past with an edifice complex wanted the world's biggest obelisk erected in his name. The problem was that the obelisk was so big, it cracked in two, whereupon the workers threw down their tools in a monumental snit fit and stomped off to drink "millions of beer," according to the hieroglyphics on the wall.

Okay, everyone back on the bus, please. Next stop, Kom Ombo down river.

If I had to choose one temple as "my favorite," it would have to be Kom Ombo, the temple to Sobek, the Crocodile God. It's not because Kom Ombo is the best temple, which it is not. Nor is it the most important temple in Egypt. Nor because it is the best preserved, which it isn't, either. In fact, Kom Ombo isn't even very old among Egypt's premier temples. It was constructed during the Greco-Roman times, which makes it practically modern day. So why was Kom Ombo so important in my memory? It is because Marty and I were on a Secret Mission to Sobek's Temple.

Six months earlier, when we were planning this trip, we decided to focus on the crocodile god because it was the sale of a large bayou in Louisiana, which I had also inherited from my cousin, that helped pay for this wonderful adventure. Louisiana bayous are literally crawling with alligators, who are first cousins to crocodiles. So, in a manner of speaking, alligators sent us across the ocean to Egypt. Marty and I felt honor-bound to show our gratitude by making a pilgrimage to Kom Ombo, the spiritual home of the VIP of toothy reptiles, Sobek, the Crocodile god, to say thank you — and to deliver a special gift from my college roommate's son, Robert.

Robert is an expert white-water rafter and kayaker. In the States, the chief outfitter for white water rafting is a company called Sobek, named after you-know-who, which manufactured special shoes for kayakers called river socks. When Robert learned that we were going to Egypt, he sent us an old pair of his Sobek river socks, and he asked us to please leave them at the temple of Kom Ombo in honor of the Crocodile God. Apparently, it is a tradition among kayakers and rafters, that, before each trip down the white water, they pour some of the water over their crafts as an offering to Sobek, the traditional river god.

Marty and I realized that we had to be very sneaky to accomplish this unusual mission. Not wanting to draw any attention to what we had in mind at this temple, we hid the shoes inside the sweatshirt that I wore. While our fellow travelers were busy snapping photos of the wall carvings in the main part of the Kom Ombo temple, Marty and I casually sauntered toward the back end of the ruin. Once alone, we looked for a niche where we could leave the shoes. Fortunately, there were several within easy reach. After shining a flashlight into one to make sure we would not disturb a sleeping snake, we stuffed Robert's river socks into the hole, and took several photographs to send to him, proving that we had accomplished his mission.

Then Marty took my hand. "Let's get out of here, before we are arrested for trashing a national monument," he muttered under his breath. We quickly returned to the temple's entrance where we rejoined our tour group. No one had missed us.

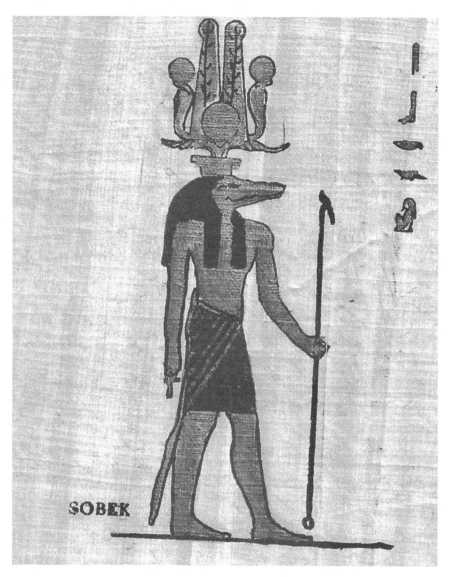

Sobek, the Crocodile God painted on modern-day papyrus
from the Papyrus Factory in Cairo.

CHAPTER TWELVE

EGYPTIAN BOOK OF THE DEAD

Further down the river (and up the map) is the town of Edfu where our boat docked after breakfast. We arrived at the front gates of the local temple hanging on for dear life inside an open-air donkey cart. It must be considered bad form to trot through the streets of the town of Edfu at a sedate pace. Everyone here galloped hell-for-leather. We were already breathless even before we had seen the first temple of the day. Edfu, with its very large, impressive gate called pylons, is dedicated to Horus, the falcon-headed god. And just inside the huge courtyard, we got to meet the Big Bird himself.

Horus's large, granite statue stood fifteen feet high, if you counted his crown which looked like a water jug balanced on the top of his feathered head. His chest was very puffed up like a pigeon's and his eyes gazed down at us with a severe expression. Lying in wait for us were several photographers who were just dying to take our photos next to Horus. Mohammed engaged in some fast price fixing, and the next thing we knew the Merry Band was hustled together for our Official Tour Group Photo. Behind us, and staring down at us, was The Bird, looking exactly like a nightmare schoolteacher giving his grade school pupils The Eye, lest someone in the front row made a face just before the shutter clicked on School Picture Day. And there we were, the Merry Band preserved for posterity – Mr. Horus' Fifth Grade at Edfu Elementary School.

Word to the Wise – every tour group that has ever set foot on the sands of Egypt since the invention of photography has posed for an official tour group photo. Some of the earliest group photos were taken of England's Prince of Wales [later Edward VII] and his party in 1862 at the temple of Karnak. The prince looked terribly bored. Picture books of Egypt are filled with two centuries' worth of tourist group photos. Don't fight it; just smile for the camera.

The next stop on our boat trip down the Nile was Esna, which is a Late Period temple that is located inside a huge hole in the ground. The most amazing thing about this building is to realize how many centuries have passed since the temple at Esna was at street level. The town of Esna, which surrounded the temple's hole, was interesting in that it was less modern than Luxor and Aswan, except for the mosque on the corniche where the Sun Boat had docked. This modern place of worship was lit up at night by dozens of multi-colored neon light strips. It was sort of a cross between a Christmas tree and a neon "Eat-at-Joe's" sign. Not exactly religious.

Moving along with the Nile's downstream current, our next stop was Deir El Bahari. Here, the magnificent funerary temple of Hatshepsut is the most unique in all of Egypt, which was a relief to us by the time we visited it. It does not look Egyptian, but Grecian in the Eighteenth Dynasty [circa 1460 BC]. Unlike all the other temples we had seen, with their huge statues and columns to match, Hatshepsut's looks like a sleek, Mediterranean summer home on the Riviera. This should not be too surprising; unlike all the other pharaohs, Hatshepsut was a woman. Men built on a colossal scale, the bigger, the better. Hatshepsut designed beauty. There is definitely a woman's touch here.

One of the most surprising things about Deir El Bahari are the painted walls. Even today, the colors remain brilliant. Looking at them, it was hard to remember that these pictures were painted over three thousand years ago. The other thing that is equally startling here, is that these priceless paintings are not behind Plexiglass nor roped off from the touch of tourists. They exist open to the air now just as they have been since the time Hatshepsut commissioned them.

Word to the wise: look, take pictures, but do not touch

Marty in front of an amazing wall painting on Queen Hatshepsut's funeral temple.
Completed in 1458 BC, the colors are still remarkably colorful.

Down river from Deir El Bahari is the legendary Valley of the Kings. This place looked like a moonscape and, even in the "cool" month of February, the dry air was very, very warm. The most famous tomb in Egypt is located here, that of the boy-king Tutankhamun, however it was closed until further notice in February 1992. The sign at the tomb's entrance said that there was a renovation in progress. However, in fact, it was closed because the sheer number of tourists trying to crowd into its four small rooms had caused the tomb's humidity to rise, and the ancient paintings were beginning to flake off the walls. While I understood and agreed with the preservation of such an important historic site, I was still disappointed not to visit inside the real tomb itself. I peered down the steps that were cut into the rock and I tried to imagine young Howard Carter at the bottom of the stairway, as he carefully broke open the priests' seals across the outer door. I pictured myself as one of the hordes of newspaper reporters, standing under the hot sun in 1922, camera in hand, waiting for the verdict.

"Tell us, Mr. Carter. What do you see?"

"Wonderful things!" he replied, which was a classic understatement.

Mary at King Tut's tomb entrance in the Valley of the Kings

Karnak – Everything that I had ever heard about the Temple of Karnak was true. Simply described – it is BIG, it's made of stone, and it is the largest place of worship in the world, including the Vatican. The hypostyle hall of enormous columns has got to be experienced to be believed.

"The first impression of Karnak is that of a palace of giants," Flaubert recorded in his diary on April 30, 1850. "As you walk about in this forest of columns, you can ask yourself whether men weren't served up whole here on skewers, like larks!"

This temple was far too large for my dazed senses to take in. After all, it was Day Eight of our Ten Glorious Days, and I was now "templed out." At this point, the only thing about Karnak that I could handle were things on a more human scale – such as the Kheper Scarab of Karnak. I realize that a three-foot long statue of a dung beetle isn't exactly on "human scale" either, but, at least, I could see the whole carving without either craning my neck or requiring Mohammed to translate it for us. By this time, our intrepid Merry Band knew that scarabs were good luck tokens, and this one was the biggest chunk of luck that we had yet seen. This scarab statue is a great favorite with the local population. He represents creation and the renewal of life. The scarab sits, in pride of place, on a four-foot-high plinth, and, if you wanted his good luck to extend to you, you must run (not walk) counter-clockwise around the plinth three times. If you wanted the added good fortune of having another child in your family during the next twelve months, you must run around this large bug seven times. This idea was very popular with hopeful grandparents.

None of our guidebooks had mentioned the Kheper Scarab of Karnak, but it was obvious from the ruts in the ground around the statue that a lot of people before us had been in search of good fortune. Well, why not? Our Merry Band were nothing if not game for anything, so everyone happily jogged three times around the scarab, much to the amusement of Mohammed and the bus driver. Meanwhile our group congratulated each other for keeping up the local tradition.

No one among the Merry Band opted for the Number Seven Jackpot.

During our entire Ten Glorious Days in Egypt, I had been on the lookout for something that fell within the realm of "exotic." By that, I meant something, preferably an animal or flower, which I had never seen, nor heard about, nor read about, nor even remotely guessed that it existed. Thanks to the Internet, television, the movies, books, magazines, and newspapers, we seem to know all there is to know about everything in the natural world. We live in an information-saturated existence. There is precious little left to truly discover. Even if someone ever catches the Loch Ness Monster, it will not be that big a surprise. We've known about the existence of this beastie for years. On this Trip of a Lifetime, I was hoping for something that would pop up which, to me, would be truly exotic.

In Luxor, I found it – or should I say, them?

Hoopoes!

I am sure that there are lots of people on this earth who know about hoopoes. For them, a hoopoe is no big deal. After all, they have probably read something about them in a National Geographic Magazine. But I, personally, had never seen, nor heard about a hoopoe. I didn't know that they existed. I never saw one at a zoo, nor in a picture book, nor on television. No one had ever said to me, "Come meet a hoopoe." Now, seeing a hoopoe for the first time was the icing on our tour cake – and they were not even included on our printed itinerary.

Hoopoes, or Whopoes, are birds about the size of a fat American robin. They have the feathering of a jaybird, only in different colors. Flaubert saw them over a hundred years ago, and he called them "tiger striped" with wings that have bold black-and-white markings in alternating bands. The bird itself is sort of a light cinnamon color with a black-and-white crest on its head. It also has a long, curved beak, black and white tail feathers, and it possesses a nasty temper. It also makes a loud, unmusical squawking noise. Hoopoes have been around for centuries in Egypt, and they are occasionally pictured or carved on the walls of tombs.

Hoopoes live up and down the Nile Valley. We spotted a pair of them on the quayside when the Sun Boat docked at Luxor. They were engaged in a noisy, all-out air attack against each other for the privilege of roosting on top of the nearby streetlight. Lurking at the base of the streetlight was a large, silent, black-and-white cat, who watched the mid-air confrontation with unwavering attention. He was waiting patiently for the loser to fall to earth. I wanted to stay and watch to see more of these wonderful birds, but Time and our Guided Tour marched on. Upon our return several hours later, both the birds and the cat were gone. I was relieved to see that there were no black-and-white feathers lying on the ground.

CHAPTER THIRTEEN

A JOURNALISTIC TOUR OF CAIRO

Day Nine found us back in Cairo, after an unadventurous flight on EgyptAir. Our tour group was checked into the Meridian Heliopolis, a French hotel, managed by a Swiss company and run by Egyptians. Day Nine also found me knocked flat by a nasty case of Pharaoh's Revenge. At least, my upset tummy waited until I was near excellent plumbing. If one is going to feel like Death Warmed Over, it is much better to do it in a good hotel, rather than on a careening tour bus.

Simple ice cubes had been my downfall – ice served in the hotel bar to chill my glass of ginger ale. Up to this point, I had been very careful about what I had put into my mouth: no raw veggies, brush teeth with bottled water, don't drink anything unless it has been boiled or an unbroken sealed bottle or both, no fish, no red meats, everything else well-cooked. Ice cubes? Chalk it up to travel fatigue.

On Day Nine in Cairo, Marty looked at me with loving sympathy, made a few comforting noises, then left for the day with Mohammed and the other members of our Merry Band who were still on their feet. The day's itinerary had the group touring Islamic Cairo. Meanwhile, I curled myself up in the middle of our bed in a pleasant, air-conditioned room.

I was accompanied by a supply of crackers, fizzy bottled water, a bottle of Imodium tablets and a day's worth of reading material.

There is nothing like a good, trashy novel and a strange newspaper in English to get one's mind off the state of one's insides. On my quick dash downstairs to the lobby shop, I had picked up a thick paperback entitled Lord of the Nile by Peter Danielson, which had a suitable sexy cover painting. The breathless back cover blurb promised the exciting story of a beautiful and courageous girl coming of age in the Eighteenth Dynasty, of the dashing, young officer in Pharaoh's army who loved the girl unto death, of the strange and violent Nubian invaders called the Black Wind, who were the most fearsome female army since the Amazons, and finally it was the story of the brave slave boy who risked his life and liberty to save the Heir of the Egyptian throne. Five hundred luscious pages of sex and violence. I put that book aside for later – like a dessert.

The English-language newspaper, The Egyptian Gazette was just what the doctor ordered: not too filling, not too fluffy and with a little meat in it. For the paltry sum of fifty piasters, about fifteen American cents, I was able to take my own private tour of Egypt, while my husband savored the mosques and minarets of Cairo. The Gazette was founded in 1880, and I now held in my hands, issue #34,627. Think of this newspaper's history! Famous world travelers such as Lawrence of Arabia, and Winston Churchill must have read copes of the Egyptian Gazette while sipping their morning tea on the verandah of the famous Shepherd's Hotel. Agatha Christie and Howard Carter must have read its news of the world while sitting in the middle of news-worthy archeological digs. Fictional sleuths Hercule Poirot and Colonel Race must have followed the local gossip in its pages as they waited for the Nile cruiser Karnak to take them to Wadi Halfa.

In 1885, the legendary British General Charles Gordon must have read, with fury, the Mahdi's defiance and later, this same newspaper would have reported Gordon's violent death at the siege of Khartoum. My favorite fictional character in Egypt, Amelia Peabody, was addicted to reading this newspaper in Cairo while waiting for her larger-than-life, archaeologist husband, Emerson, to return from yet another noisy confrontation with the officials of the Egyptian Antiquities Museum. And now, here I was, embarking on the same literary adventure while curled up in bed in the Meridian Heliopolis Hotel.

As one would expect, the front page was dominated by news of the Middle East with such datelines as Cairo, Addis Ababa, Dakar, Amman, Kabul, Tel Aviv, Djibouti, Nicosia, and, of course, the United Nations. Such a roll call fairly reeks of Arabian Nights. The only front-page story from the United States did not deal with President George Bush's bid for re-election, but instead, it was an obituary for Ettie Mae Greene of Lindeside, West Virginia, who had just died at the advanced age of 114 years. She had been the oldest living American I could not imagine my hometown newspaper, the Washington Post, running this tidbit on their front page. If the late Mrs. Greene had been lucky, she might have been listed on the Post's back pages of the Metro Section under "Obits."

On the other hand, the big local news in Cairo, and other parts of the Arab world, was the coming of Ramadan, the month of fasting and prayers for all Muslims. The editors of the Gazette solemnly exhorted their readers to keep the month of Ramadan from turning into "an opportunity for laziness, sleep and vacations." No secular American newspaper would dare to print any comments about the observance of Christian Lent or Jewish Yom Kippur, much less presume to lecture its readers how to behave during a time of prayers and penance. Yet in Egypt, this was front page news as well as the lead editorial.

The other editorials in the Gazette were well-thought out, and they gave me a different insight of the two mighty forces in the world today, the United States and the former Soviet Union. Both countries have a high impact upon Egypt. If the United States sneezes, the Egyptians stock up on Kleenex. I found it interesting that the editorial on the U.S. was lifted verbatim from a recent New York Times article. Upon further reflection,

I found it even more interesting to realize that Egypt rarely appears on the editorial page of the Post. Egypt's problems with its exploding population and its unstable politics are huge, but internal. The average American couldn't care a thing, unless he was planning to travel to Egypt soon. Then, and only then, will the self-blinkered American be interested in what the temperature is in Cairo, what the exchange rate is and whether there has been any terrorist activity recently which could affect his Trip of a Lifetime. It is a shame that we Americans fail to realize that we are citizens of the world. The Gazette, in its mere eight pages, exuded more of a world awareness than I have ever experienced reading my "major" Washington Post newspaper back home. Not only did the Gazette report news bytes from the Arab-African sphere – a huge area – but there were also stories about the European Common Market, India, Viet-Nam, Bangkok, Dublin's recent IRA activity, and Yugoslavia. There was only one story on the USA's upcoming presidential election from Houston, Texas.

It is interesting to realize that the Egyptians, poor, often illiterate Third World citizens, are more knowledgeable of the world at large than we, well-educated and self-satisfied folk are in the US. In the past Eight Glorious Days of our Egyptian adventure, I had been struck by the sheer number of tourists who, speaking in a variety of languages, flooded this country daily. The Egyptians, always smiling, responded to all, often in the visitors' own language. Most Egyptians can understand a bit of English, as well as French, German, Spanish and Japanese. This is something most of Americans cannot do, and worse, we take national pride in our ignorance. We expect everyone whom we meet to speak English, and we brand those who do not as "simple foreigners."

I must admit that I do like the Washington Post. It is my breakfast-time companion, and it does carry News of the World – but that is buried deep in the middle pages where most Post readers never look. The Post is far too large for a complete daily read-through, unless one happens to be independently wealthy and does not have to fight commuter traffic twice a day. One must be retired to have all day to study the Post from cover to cover. The Washington Post, the "most important newspaper in the most important city in the world", usually has twenty pages in each section and four or five sections in each daily issue, Sundays not included. The Sunday editions can swell to over a hundred pages of mostly advertising.

The plucky little Egyptian Gazette, issue #34,627, was only eight pages in length – four double sides, two folded sheets. Which daily newspaper would the harried commuter be more likely to read from cover to cover as he or she gulps down boiling morning coffee?

The Gazette had it all: movie listings (all American films during this week), a crossword puzzle, a bridge and chess game section, sports – one page only – the television and radio schedules (with special emphasis on the religious programming), the weather report, the gold and silver world market prices and only two ads for apartments to rent. Sadly, there are no comic strips, nor editorial cartoons, but there were a clever artist's renderings of Cairo's daily life under the title "Weekly Sketches." Today's artwork was titled "The Scale" – drawings of the street vendors who carry around scales to weigh passers-by for a few piasters each.

The report on movie actress Elizabeth Taylor's 60th birthday party took up two columns – more news coverage than given the rest of the United States combined. Of course, Liz Taylor once portrayed Cleopatra in a mega-movie of the same name, so that might have something to do with the enthusiastic press. Also, the Egyptians, primarily the men, just love Liz.

I found that the paper's proofreaders were a little relaxed. "Speech" was spelled "spxeech" and "evening" appeared as "eving", but, after all, English is the second language for most of the paper's staff and readers as well. While the copy's grammar was occasionally fractured, overall, I liked the Gazette very much. If nothing else, it made me realize that the United States is not the hub of the world. And reading it took my mind off my tummy.

CHAPTER FOURTEEN

A TRAVELER IN AN ANTIQUE LAND

"Everything in Egypt seems made for archenteric," Flaubert observed in his book. "The whole country is a massive artwork sitting on top of an endless sand pile. There are temples, colossi, mud-brick villages, donkeys, tomb paintings, camels, beautiful children, and fiery dawns. There seems to be no separation between the past and the present. They both exist side-by-side."

Looking back on our Ten Glorious Days in Egypt, I am surprised to realize that the things I had journeyed so far to see, and which I had fully expected to love, didn't excite me too much. Meanwhile, the unplanned and unexpected surprises, for the most part, were wonderful.

For instance, there were the Pyramids, the greatest construction project ever completed by mankind. I wanted to be impressed, to be awestruck, to be uplifted. I wasn't. From a distance, they looked like all the pictures that I had ever seen of them, starting with that Camel cigarette package artwork. Up close, they appeared to be a wall of endless stone, and I went away, disappointed. It was not until our departing airplane rose over Cairo and we looked down on the pyramids from the air that we saw their relationship to the modern city nearby. Only then could I really appreciate the vast area they covered. Still, all things considered, they were not what I had expected, and I missed that feeling.

That other Egyptian icon, the Sphinx, was also a disappointment. I was prepared for it to look small next to the Pyramids – there were enough warnings in the guidebooks – but I was not prepared for its sad state of deterioration. True, we only saw it by the fast-fading purple sunset, and its face — so enigmatic – was almost invisible amid the violet shadows. No contours, no facial line, no soul – just a large mass of stone with scaffolding on one side.

On the other hand, the ride on the camel was fantastic! Wonderful! Perfect! Exciting! And – relaxing. Such a slow, rhythmic sway! After a jam-packed day of sightseeing, according to the Gospel of Tour Itinerary, our brief ride on Fatima's back was so restful and scenic. Onward, Fatima, glorious beast! Approaching the pyramids from the desert side, away from the mobs of tourists and fleets of sight-seeing buses, I gave myself up to the camel's rolling motion, while I dreamed of Arabian nights. Fatima, you were worth every piaster, even though you did want to take us on a side trip to Libya.

Finally, just before our tour bus left the Giza Plateau, when we had seen all the Great Sights, and when the misty, violet twilight stole softly in from the vastness of the Great Western Desert, there was a lone rider upon his camel, who paused at the base of a sand dune, in the lee of a palm tree. In that magic moment, time stood still. That one moment, and the memory of my childhood desire that it conjured up, took away my breath as no giant triangle of stone ever did.

Getting to Abu Simbel was a series of "hurry up and wait . . . wait . . . wait" thanks to EgyptAir. It was twilight again and there was much grumbling among our Merry Band for fear that all their Photo Opportunities would be lost to darkness. But Rameses the Great worked his own magic. As the evening drew in, turning Lake Nasser 's waters purple and the sky pink, the sudden wash of illumination lit up the gigantic king, bathing His

Majesty in its golden glow. Deep within his shrine, the golden glow of the holy of holies sprang awake like a welcoming beacon. The power and the aura of this most egotistical monarch was palpable. We could taste the mystery of the place in the very air. The massive stone figures assumed an inner warmth, their eyes watchful. Only hushed voices accompanied our awe of that moment – lest the magic would flee away. It was beautiful, breathtaking. It was an experience unexpected.

On the other hand, the storied Valley of the Kings was mostly "Closed for Renovation." Exactly how does one "renovate" a valley? I tried to be excited as we descended into one of the few bona fide Egyptian tombs currently open to view. Shades of Boris Karloff in his ragged mummy wrappings came to mind. I listened for the voices of explorers Peabody and Emerson as they conducted their studies in a distant painted hallway – but, alas, the spark that had blazed so brightly at Abu Simbel fizzled in the Valley of the Kings. Did the hundreds of tourists scare away the ghosts of Ancient Egypt?

After several days of non-stop temple viewing, they all started to look alike, which was why Hatshepsut's tomb was so refreshingly different – except that it too was "Closed for Renovation." Instead, we stumbled among the columns and looked at the flaking painted walls.

After all, the paint had been on those walls for over thirty-five hundred years. Tourists are supposed to be excited by this artwork, but I fear that I have a serious problem with ancient Egyptian interior decoration. As a modern-day designer would put it, the walls were far too "busy." Perhaps I should have been thankful that everything was not completely painted in the bright colors they once had been. My eyes would have gone into shock if they had. Of all the hundreds of painted walls that we saw, the one I liked best was the simple, starry sky on the ceiling at Abu Simbel. It was just a blue background with golden, five-pointed stick-like stars, row upon row. I found them very restful.

Ever since I saw that wonderful opening scene from the 1945 movie *Caesar and Cleopatra*, when Vivian Leigh nestled between the paws of the great Sphinx, I had always dreamed of being in a similar position. Naturally, the current sad state of the Sphinx, with the barriers and scaffolding around it, made it impossible to realize that dream. However, in a manner of speaking, I did get my Sphinx wish after all.

There was a charming little pink granite Sphinx lying by a papyrus-ringed pond in front of Cairo's Museum of Antiquities. He was very approachable and, more to the point, he was a size that completely fit inside a camera's viewfinder. It was very nice to sit beside him and stroke his paw for good luck. This was Egyptian Art and History – up close and personal.

By and large – and everything seemed to be large in Egypt except the beautiful children and the sweet little donkeys – I liked the statues best of all. The top two on my list of stony friends are Horus, the falcon god at Edfu, and the scarab at the temple of Karnak. I never expected to be excited over a bug, especially a big bug, but this scarab was exceptional as well as approachable.

Egypt is a land of contrasts: stone, rocks, and blistering sand on one side of the river, while deep green fields of clover, bananas and sugar cane grew on the other. Most of the people outside of Cairo live in mud-brick villages without indoor plumbing or any sort of modern sanitation. Instead of a car in the non-existent driveway, a patient donkey is tethered to the doorpost.

There must be rich Egyptians at the top of the social ladder, but they stay well out-of-sight, barricaded behind high walls, and protected by personal armed guards. The overwhelming majority of the local population are poor, although not in spirit. It was no wonder that everyone we met, especially the winsome children, wanted our money. There was always a hand outstretched, a gentle rubbing of fingers and a soft murmuring of "baksheesh, baksheesh" – share your wealth. After a short while, it became too easy to ignore them, to look through them. Yet the people were always there – everywhere – softly murmuring.

Do they hate us, the rich tourists who wander through their land, much like the Romans did two thousand years ago? Do they envy our perceived wealth? We have traveled thousands of miles to visit Egypt, and travel is very expensive, especially for ones who cannot afford more than one donkey. Travel is for the rich; travel is an exotic pastime. That is why those Egyptians who have made a "haj", the religious pilgrimage to Mecca, paint the outside walls of their houses with scenes of their trip, including their mode of transportation, such as airplanes.

Do the Egyptians hate us foreigners who walk around as if we owned the place? Yet the children in the fields with their shy smiles and melting chocolate eyes wave wildly at us as we zoom by in our air-conditioned tour bus. They get so excited if we wave back to them. The eternal peddlers of beads, statues and postcards who dogged our steps from Saqqara to Abu Simbel were cheerful, even if we did not buy any of their wares. They did not curse or swear at our retreating backs. They made a joke instead.

"Look at this tambourine, lady, just look – one pound!"

Naturally you look at it and the vendor laughs. "See? You looked! Now you pay me one pound!" and everyone laughs because he is only kidding. This is the Egyptian sense of humor.

Absolutely everything seems to take longer to accomplish in Egypt. "The Egyptian temperament accepts delay with a shrug and a murmured reference to the will of Allah," wrote novelist Elizabeth Peters, who is also a professional Egyptologist, ". . . the most frequently heard word in the Egyptian vocabulary is 'bukra' (tomorrow)." We Westerners make great efforts to be efficient, organized and get things done quickly, but in doing so, have we forgotten how to take pleasure in the art of living? Service is teeth-grindingly slow in the restaurants; all the better to make conversation, of course. EgyptAir's timetable is a work of fiction. There is only one thing you can be sure of about EgyptAir: they will arrive or depart only when Allah wills it.

Nothing is accomplished without a great deal of cigarette smoking and rapid-fire discussion involving as many people as possible. At the very least, the average Egyptian man does not suffer from a communications gap. Interestingly, it is only the men who do all the talking in public. Women, especially out in the countryside, are hardly ever seen, much less heard.

It was a cultural shock to do business with the charming perfume bottle seller in Luxor, but, as she shyly pointed out to us, she was a Coptic Christian and was not bound by the Islamic laws regarding women.

When we tourists went into the towns to do a little shopping, loud bargaining and bewildering the Americans was the name of the game. The souks and bazaars were both tempting and terrifying at the same time. The vendors were never shy. Why should they be? They wanted our business and were out to get it before the vendor at the next stall attracted our attention. With no time to think or choose wisely, our Merry Band was often caught in a cultural crossfire. While the Western part of our brains kept whispering that we had to be back on the tour bus in five minutes, the Eastern part was looking forward to a lively and engaging bargaining exchange. Admittedly, most of us often wound up seated in our plush bus seats not sure exactly what we had just purchased, nor how much our new item had cost us in "real money", i.e., American dollars.

Speaking of money, Egyptian money doesn't look real. Instead, it looks like something that was borrowed from a Monopoly game, and then had been left outside for several days in the rain and sun. New pound notes of any domination were as rare as the proverbial hen's teeth. It was a general feeling among our group that there was no such thing as an Egyptian coin, until someone on Day Nine got a few in change. The rest of us gazed at the little aluminum disks in his hand with the same wonder and awe as we had given the Pyramids. Incidentally, one Egyptian pound in 2023 was equal to thirty-three American pennies.

Our stay in Egypt was only Ten Glorious Days – most of that time was spent on the run. Was there enough time for us to understand everything that we had experienced during that short time? Or was it easier for us to complain? The planes are late. The tour bus is late. You can't just pay for something and leave. There's no toilet paper in the restrooms. On the other hand, what is the point of traveling if we want everything to be "just like home?"

We tourists, who arrive in Egypt in droves and who speak in an assortment of languages, want to change Egypt the minute we land in Cairo. "What this place needs . . .," we said every ten minutes. Yet, we had traveled thousands of miles to visit the country known as "The Mother of Civilization." Western visitors are full of suggestions for home improvements. "Put an escalator in the Great Pyramid." "Get the EgyptAir baggage handlers to stop talking and start moving our stuff." "Expand, enlarge and revamp the Gift Shop in the Museum of Antiquities." "Clean up, re-arrange and redesign the million objects in the Museum itself." "Put a McDonalds at Aswan, at Giza, and at Abu Simbel." "Widen the roads." "Control the traffic." And finally, "Get all those kids on the roadside into some shoes and put them in school!" Welcome to the Middle East!

The Bible tells us that the meek shall inherit the earth. No doubt, Egypt will continue to plod along on her donkeys long after our civilization has descended into concrete dust. Egypt has seen civilizations come and go: Greek, Roman, Islamic, French, English, American. Who is to say which way of life is better in the long, long run? Who really cares anyway? Things will change tomorrow, insha'allah mumkin bukra.

Minarets on a Cairo Mosque.

APPENDIX

WHAT YOU SHOULD KNOW BEFORE YOU GO

SUGGESTED PACKING LIST FOR TEN GLORIOUS DAYS IN EGYPT

Winter months are the best time to go to Egypt. The country is in the Northern Hemisphere, so winter is from December to March. Wintertime temps in Egypt are cool, like autumn in the USA. Keep in mind you will be traveling in a foreign country and far outside your normal comfort zone.

Note: Egypt is a Moslem country and very conservative in dress, particularly for women. General rule of thumb for both men and women: do not show bare arms above the elbows, nor any bare legs. Women should not wear tight-fitting shirts or pants. Never wear shorts. You will want to take most of the following:

- 12 pairs of underwear [6 or 7 bras for the women]

- 14 pairs of socks

- 1 set of pajamas or flannel nightgown – suitable to be seen outside the boat's cabin stateroom in case of an emergency. Nothing sexy or see-thru.

- Bedroom slippers – boats and hotels in Cairo are kept clean, but Egypt has a huge population of scorpions, spiders, and venomous snakes. All of them can squeeze under closed doors. Bare feet and open sandals are not a great idea anywhere or any time in Egypt. Always shake out your shoes and slippers before you put them on.

- 2-3 pairs of loose, comfortable, cotton or cotton-blend long pants – check out L.L. Bean.

- I wore black and kakis long pants with elastic waistbands and deep slash pockets.

- 3-4 long-sleeved shirts – I wore long sleeve, Oxford shirts. Nothing tight. No tees.

- 1 woolen sweater – desert evenings are cool.

- 1 sweatshirt – be careful that your sweatshirt does not have any human figure on it, nor any religious symbols, nor any crass wording on it.

- One semi-dressy outfit for the get-acquainted dinner and the boat's "formal" evening. No bare arms, shoulders, and no cleavage showing even on the boat or at a modern hotel. The waiters are all Muslims. Bathing suits are okay, but only poolside. Wear a wrap-up robe to and from your cabin or hotel room.

- 2 pairs of thick-soled shoes suitable for walking over packed sand and uneven ground. Most everyone on our tour wore some sort of sport shoe. We also wore leather shoes with thick crepe soles.

- A hat with a wide brim that goes all the way around to protect the back of the neck from the sun. Cotton or straw hats are best. Ball caps are useless in the desert sun. I wore a lightweight, white straw pith helmet or solar topee. I found it in a funny little store in Annapolis, MD. Amazon.com features inexpensive pith helmets. Make sure you get one that has an inner headband with a terry cloth liner across the forehead. The most common hat for tourists is the bucket hat which is often sold in hotel shops and on the boats.

- A medium – weight jacket or trench coat for the very cool days in northern Egypt.

- A pair of light-weight gloves if you plan to ride a camel. You will be hanging on either the saddle pommel or a rough single rein. Gloves are a must, especially if you plan to pat the camel.

- A flat, water bottle with carrying strap. Fill only with fresh bottled water.

- A bandana – not necessary, but very handy to soak up sweat around your neck or to use as an impromptu shopping bag or as a mask against dust.

- A money pouch that you wear as a belt or hanging around your neck inside your shirt. Pickpockets abound, especially in markets and bazaars.

- Note: do not wear eye-catching jewelry anywhere. Wear a plain, inexpensive wristwatch and only wedding rings. No flashy engagement rings. No rings with any jewel-like stone in them.

- Sunscreen lotion for the face, neck, and arms – use it every day.

- Insect repellent – not necessary in the winter months from December to March, but very necessary the rest of the time.

- Lip balm – sun, wind and dry weather will crack your lips. You are in desert country.

- Clear eye drops/artificial tears – good for sunbaked eyes.

- Sunglasses – either prescription or plain. No fashion brands to attract thieves.

- 6 – 12 white hankies.

- Always carry a roll of camper's TP and a pocket flashlight with extra batteries with you.

- Do not carry large handbags anywhere. It only announces your wealth. Wear pants with deep pockets, like cargo pants or jackets with inside pockets.

- Pack a mini first aid kit – just in case.

- Put all medicines in your carry-on bag on the plane.

DO'S AND DON'T'S WHEN TRAVELING IN EGYPT

- Do take a trip to Egypt at least once in your lifetime. Egypt is the mother country for "Western" civilization as well as Eastern.

- Do use a good travel agent to book your hotels, travel connections and, most importantly, your Nile cruise boat. Make these arrangements about three months before you wish to leave. Be aware of the current political situation in Egypt. Check online for the U. S. State Department's most recent travel advisory for Egypt.

- Do take a reputable, all-inclusive guided Nile River cruise. It is the best and safest way to see Ancient Egypt. Also, it is a lot of fun. Most cruises last five days and four nights. You can book longer tours, but they are much more expensive. We used Abercrombie & Kent tours.

- Do go during the winter months, i.e., November through March. Egypt is north of the Equator and therefore in the Northern hemisphere. The temperatures are the best and the insect population is asleep, for the most part.

- Do make an appointment with your doctor about two months before your trip to get the appropriate inoculations and renewal of necessary prescriptions that you will need during your journey. Imodium is a very good idea to have on hand. Also, a first aid kit for any scratches you get.

- Do use an antiseptic like Neosporin on any cut, scratch, or open wound as soon as possible. Pack a tube to take with you.

- Do read books about Egypt, both modern and ancient. The more you know about ancient Egypt, the more you will enjoy what you are seeing. [Reading list is further on]. Highly recommended is an

English translation, with photographs, of the Egyptian Book of the Dead.

- Do learn the basics of the Islamic religion. Most of the people of Egypt practice this religion and they are offended if visitors dress or act in ways that they consider irreligious. Be respectful of their religious practices, even if they are inconvenient or seem sexist to you.

- Do be polite always, no matter what. You are a guest in Egypt; use your good manners.

- Do take a ride on a camel by the Pyramids. It will be one of those experiences that you will talk about for years afterward.

- Do bargain when shopping in markets and bazaars. Once you get the hang of it, you may find it's a lot of fun. That is the whole point. Egyptians will respect you better if you bargain.

- Do always wear a hat and/or use an umbrella or parasol when outside, even on cloudy days. The sunshine in Egypt is strong and can be deadly.

- Do always pay attention of your surroundings. Listen to your instincts. If you feel uncomfortable in your surroundings, then leave quickly.

- Do always stick with your tour group, even if they are traveling at a snail's pace. Always let your tour guide as well as your friends, know where you are going – i.e., to the restroom – and, if possible, always have someone with you. Move about in pairs.

- Do crawl up inside the Great Pyramid if that option is still offered. Yes, it's a little scary, but well-worth the experience and the expense. It's a real Indiana Jones moment. Recently, the Egyptian Tourist Board has built an ascending stairway with permanent handrails in the Great Pyramid. Much easier than the ladder.

- Do use sunscreen and insect repellent., even on cloudy days.

- Do carry some American dollars with you. Many places in the markets and bazaars don't have credit card readers. Keep all your money out of sight and hidden on your person – never in your hip pocket.

- Do carry a small flashlight and batteries with you at all times. You will be glad that you did.

- Pause for a few words about my second-best friend in Egypt – my precious roll of camper's toilet paper. This type of toilet paper doesn't come with a cardboard roll in the center. Camper's toilet looks like the cardboard was extracted by pliers and then an elephant stomped on it until the roll was flattened. Then the wad was folded, lengthwise, so that it could fit inside a side pocket on a backpack, or as in my case, inside a deep pants pocket.

- If you look up "camper's toilet paper" on Google, you will find a bewildering plethora of products. For an item that is as personal and as important as toilet paper, it is advisable that you visit a camping store like REI in person. You are not looking for something that is listed "biodegradable". Most of the time, this phrase means that the paper sooner or later dissolves when wet, and this is something you don't want to mess with, literally. In fact, you probably will not be outside while answering the calls of nature. There is absolutely no place like a woodsy area wherein to discreetly hide what you are doing when you are sightseeing in the Egyptian desert. Also, it is the height of bad manners, not to mention against the law, if you poop inside a tomb. There are hidden security cameras everywhere in the Valleys of the Kings and Queens. And you certainly don't want a camera-crazy fellow traveler like George catching you in the act. At most of the sightseeing areas, you will probably find some sort of shack wherein quick-dissolving biodegradable toilet paper is not necessary for the safety of the local environment. You will want personal comfort. We are talking about your tender skin here. Egyptian TP is like wax paper.

- There are approximately 140 sheets in the average roll of camper's TP, no matter which brand you choose. I managed to get through a full week of sightseeing with just one roll, though I did have a second roll in my suitcase. Camper's TP isn't expensive, so buy two rolls – just in case. You never know when Pharoah's Revenge is going to hit. Also, always carry a small squeeze bottle of hand sanitizer, like Purell, with you. It will save you from a world of discomfort.

Now back to the "Don't's" —-

- Don't wander away from your tour group, no matter how boring/ stupid/or embarrassing they may be. Never go off on your own to shop or sightsee. Stick with your group. Never go anywhere with some one you don't know, even if it's just around the corner to check out a vendor's stall.

- Don't wear tight clothing. Don't bare your arms above your elbows, don't wear short shorts, or tight leggings. Your clothing choices might offend the Egyptians or send a signal that you have loose morals. Ladies, no workout clothing, please. You are asking to get pinched in the backside.

- Don't be disrespectful of the habits and/or customs of the Egyptian people. Always be on your best behavior.

- Don't speak in loud voices when out in public. Don't criticize the Egyptian people or their way of life out loud. Most Egyptians speak some English.

- Don't ever, ever pet, pick up, stroke, or hold any animal, alive or dead, in Egypt. They are crawling with all sorts of bugs, literal and biological. Don't hold a tiny monkey for a photograph; they tend to bite or crap on you – or both. Don't pet the donkeys or camels. Wear gloves when you are outside. Don't put your hands or feet in the Nile, no matter how inviting the water looks. It's loaded with nasty bacteria, not to mention the rare lurking crocodile.

- Don't drink any water in Egypt unless you see that it comes in a bottle with an unbroken seal. The Westerner's tender stomach is no match for Middle Eastern water supplies. You will be deathly sick. Also, beware of ice cubes, even in the best hotels.

- Don't feed any animal in Egypt. They bite and medical attention is sketchy at best.

- Don't make rude comments in English, French, Spanish, German, or any other language. Most Egyptians understand rude and crude words in a variety of languages, and they will take instant offense if they hear you whispering scathing remarks about themselves. Yes, they will understand you and be gravely offended.

- Don't try to cheat shopkeepers or venders at bazaars, markets, or souvenir shops. First, they know all the tricks of the trade and then some. Second, they have an excellent grasp on how much their wares are worth in a variety of different currencies. Third, no matter how clever you think you are at getting "a deal", the shop keepers and vendors are the experts at the art of buying, selling, and bargaining.

- Don't eat any raw fruit or vegetable, no matter how enticing it looks. The farmers use human waste products as fertilizer on their crops.

- Don't insist on women's rights in Egypt. Women's lib and "girl power" doesn't work here and will only attract the wrong, and possibly dangerous kind of attention from the Egyptians of both sexes. Dress modestly, keep your voices low, and stick with your tour group. Always remember that you are guest in Egypt, even if you are paying thousands of dollars to visit here.

- Don't sit on, stand on or even lean on any ancient stone carving or statue. If every tourist did this, the ancient stones would soon wear away to nothing.

- Don't try to climb up the outside of a pyramid. Not only is it highly dangerous, but it is also highly illegal. You can spend three years in an Egyptian jail for trying it.

- Don't go outside during the daylight hours without a hat. Sunstroke gives no warning; it just happens.

- Don't flash your money around. Don't pull out a wad of bills to count out the price of the item you are buying. You are asking for a fast theft.

- Don't put your money, wallet, passport, ID card, credit cards, hotel room key, or phone in your hip or back pocket. Pickpockets abound and they are fast. Even the most charming of children can whisk away your wallet faster than the blink of an eye. Divide your day's spending money into several locations on your person, so that you don't pull out a large amount of money to pay for something.

- Don't forget where you are spending the night. Write down the name and address of your hotel, if you are in a city, or the name and company of your Nile cruiser and keep that paper in a safe pocket.

- Don't buy anything made of ivory or crocodile skin. These items are prohibited to import into the USA and there is a heavy fine if you try it. And yes, the US Customs inspectors are on the lookout for these particular items.

- Don't take a picture of any Egyptian, especially children, unless you ask permission first. You may have to pay a little tip for the permission.

- Note on photography: Most people will tend to use their phone cameras. This is good, if you don't lose your phone, run out of power at the wrong time or if you want to take very detailed, artist-quality photographs. Be sure to take LOTS of photos. In later years, you will be glad you did. In 1992, we used real cameras with spool film. Our slides, negatives and photos have not faded over the decades. If you are planning to use your phone's camera, you should make hard copy prints as soon as possible. These will keep longer in your photo albums than on your phone. Single use, disposable cameras are making a comeback. If you don't want to invest in an expensive film camera, the disposables are a good choice to take to Egypt.

- Finally, always, always remember that when you are in Egypt, you are representing the United States of America. For some Egyptians, you may be the very first American that they have ever encountered. They will judge our country by your behavior.

SHOPPING!

There is an enormous number of things you can buy in Egypt, at all prices and quality. It is very much a "buyer beware" market. Use your common sense.

Souvenirs:

Beads – there are bead sellers everywhere. Beads make nice gifts for hard-to-please distant aunts, second-best friends, or little girls. There are also the more expensive beads made of lapis lazuli and turquoise. You will have to be able to tell the difference between the real and the fake. Beads are the easiest things to pack.

Earrings are fun and come in all shapes, sizes, colors, and materials. No crocodile teeth, please. Be sure to wipe down the earrings with alcohol before use.

Gold jewelry. Again, know what you are looking for and be able to tell the real thing from the fake.

Mother-of-pearl inlaid boxes in all sizes. These are nice, relatively inexpensive and make lovely gifts, for yourself and/or others.

Glass perfume bottles come in all sizes and colors. They are beautiful, relatively inexpensive, but very fragile. Need to be well-wrapped to get back to home in one piece.

Statuettes in all sizes, prices, and shapes. Very popular are the black stone cats, for Bastet, the Cat goddess. All your cat-loving friends will adore them. Ditto the jackal god of the dead, Anubis, for your dog-loving friends. The falcon god, Horus, looks good on anyone's desk. Little scarabs about the size of a fifty-cent piece are fun to give as gifts to just about everyone you know. Everyone could use a bit of good luck. There are King Tut's and Queen Nefertiti's, as well as just about anything Egyptian. The prices are good, and bargaining is fun. These statuettes pack well and are non-breakable unless you accidently step on them.

Wood is scarce in Egypt, but a wooden camel adds a bit of the Middle East to a Christmas Nativity set. Ditto brass camels or camel bells.

Rugs are a nice gift, for yourself or others, and the easiest type of rugs to take home are the traditional prayer rugs. They are small, good for hallways or as spot rugs for color. They are also easier to pack for the trip home.

Perfumes are stronger than you may be used to, and the prices vary.

Do not be tempted to buy spices, most are not allowed to be imported in the USA. Also, spices that are not sealed in a non-breakable container will be hell-on-earth to get out of clothing or your suitcase if the container breaks open during the trip home.

Brass hubbly bubbly water pipes come apart easily for packing and once you understand how they work back home, you and your friends might enjoy smoking them. Also, water pipes make interesting, decorative items to perch on sideboards and brag about.

Papyrus pictures are modern-day paintings of ancient Egyptian scenes on modern-day manufactured papyrus. They come in all sizes and keep well once they are framed. They are not ancient relics, but they are made in Cairo. Papyrus bookmarks are inexpensive, unique, easy to pack, lightweight, and everyone back home will want one. Buy extras.

Note: Do not buy anything that claims to be from an ancient tomb. It is illegal to take authentic ancient Egyptian artifacts out of the country without going through a lot of paperwork and expense.

SUGGESTED READING LIST

Insight Guides: The Nile, Guidebook, edited and produced by Andrew Eames; APA Publications, LTD. This book covers it all: history, sites, places to visit; maps; illustrated with color photographs. 300 pages.

Note: A good guidebook to Egypt and the Nile is highly recommended.

Death on the Nile, mystery by Agatha Christie.

Note: The movie, Death on the Nile, starring Peter Ustinov & Mia Farrow is an excellent way to preview the Nile River sites as well as Nile cruise boats. The Nile cruisers are quite safe; there has never been a real murder on board any of them to date, but it is fun to pretend that you are on Agatha Christie's death-ridden boat, the Karnak.

Crocodile on the Sandbank, mystery by Elizabeth Peters.

New York: Dodd, Mead & Company; 1992.

Note: This is the first book in Amelia Peabody Egyptian mystery series by Elizabeth Peters.

The Egyptian Book of the Dead; translated by Raymond O. Faulkner; New York: Fall River Press; 2003.

Note: there are several different translations of the Book of the Dead. All of them are good.

Tutankhamun: Life and Death of a Pharaoh; by Christine Desroches-Noblecourt; New York: Doubleday; 1965.

Note: There are a lot of books on King Tutankhamen, most of them are well-written.

On The Nile: In the Golden Age of Travel, by Andrew Humphreys; The American University of Cairo Press; Cairo & New York; 2015. All about the Nile River Cruise Boats from 1880 through the 1940s.

Note: A trip to your local Library to look up books on Egypt will give you enough reading material for a year. This list is merely a guide to the most interesting subjects.

Rubaiyat of Omar Khayyam; translated by Edward FitzGerald; New York, Random House; 1947. This is not Egyptian, but it is a beautiful insight into Arabian poetry.

Innocents Abroad by Mark Twain; a wonderful adventure story with a great deal of humor, especially the chapter on Egypt.

ACKNOWLEDGEMENTS

The author is deeply indebted to her friends Virginia and Harry Day for proof-reading and fact-checking this manuscript. Also, there is a much-belated thank you to the members of the Merry Band who took so many photos of our memorable camel ride. As it is now over thirty years since our Ten Glorious Day in Egypt, the author has no idea who took which photos of us on Fatima. Therefore, here is a blanket thank you to all twenty-four of you. Our complete set of camel photos fills many pages of our photo album. Last, but never least, thank you to my patient and loving husband, Marty Schaller, who spent hours hunched over the computer capturing all our pre-cellphone photo images and inserting them into the manuscript.

Mary W. Schaller in the Kitchener Gardens, Aswan, Egypt 1992.
Photo by Martin Schaller

ABOUT THE AUTHOR

Mary W. Schaller, better known to millions of readers as Harlequin Romance writer Tori Phillips, was born in Washington, DC and she remains staunchly non-partisan for survival. In 1965, she earned her Bachelor of Arts Degree from the University of San Diego, California where she studied Ancient Egyptian Civilization, writing her thesis on the Egyptian Book of the Dead. She is the author of ten Harlequin Romances that have sold over two and a half million copies worldwide. Her three non-fiction books about the American Civil War and World War I, are published by the University of South Carolina Press and have won several awards. Her five plays, published by Dramatic Publishing Company and Heartland Plays, have been performed not only across the United States, but also in Canada, Australia, and England. Mary and her husband, Marty live in Springfield, VA, and they have recently celebrated fifty-nine years of marriage and adventures. They are the parents of two charming adults, and the grandparents of three fascinating young people. For relaxation, Mary and Marty love to read lots of books, travel on cruise ships and enjoy James Bond and Indiana Jones movies.